HIDDEN HISTORY

HISTORY

of

SAVANNAH

HIDDEN
HISTORY
of
SAVANNAH

Brenna Michaels and T.C. Michaels

Published by The History Press
Charleston, SC
www.historypress.com

Copyright © 2019 by Brenna Michaels and T.C. Michaels
All rights reserved

First published 2019

Manufactured in the United States

ISBN 9781467141123

Library of Congress Control Number: 2018960963

For Rhett. To know where you've come from.

CONTENTS

PREFACE

It's hard to imagine a place that could get under your skin quite like Savannah. It's more than the picturesque squares, the cobblestones or the moss-draped branches. There's a nobility that hangs on the air. The past walks hand in hand with the present, leaping to life every time someone pauses to remember.

And there's so much to be remembered. The souls who planted this old place beside the ocean more than two hundred years ago. The brothers and sisters who shot up on this American soil and dreamed new dreams, unleashed by freedom and fresh starts and driven on by bravery and gumption the like the world has rarely seen since.

The names of famous and not-so-famous settlers are still granted to newborn Savannah babies. Its street names echo the birthrights of fallen war heroes and controversial governors alike. The conglomeration of culture and foreign blood brought together in the pursuit of happiness makes up the heartbeat of this vibrant place.

And while to walk Savannah's streets today feels something like stepping into a fairytale, it has been a long road to bring it here. As with all beautiful stories, good intentions have met with tragedy, beauty has sometimes been swallowed up by the beast and the struggle to make it past dark nights into morning has, at times, been nearly too much to bear. And yet time and again, Savannah emerged from each new challenge more stalwart, more beautiful and more treasured than before.

In writing this book, we have made every effort to honor the notable and the not-so-well-remembered histories of our exquisite home of Savannah. Living and working and raising our child in the historic district has been one of the blessings of our life, and we hope to have recounted the lesser-told stories of this place into a work that can be enjoyed by anyone and everyone.

As public historians and professional storytellers within our Savannah-based business, Genteel & Bard, we have done our best to bring forth the most accurate and interesting representations of Savannah's rather storied and sometimes convoluted past. We would like to thank the Georgia Historical Society, the Historic Savannah Foundation and all the many Savannah natives and academic professionals who have had a hand in aiding our research.

What a blessing to dive deeper into familiar waters. Welcome to Savannah, y'all. We're so happy to share it with you.

INTRODUCTION

It was a dream that, by all accounts, never should have come true. Time and again, this city of Savannah stood on the edge of ruin, brought to its knees by bloody battles, mysterious pestilence, fire, unforgiving weather and the drums of war.

Once seen as an undesirable hovel, the unlikely Gem of the South became known as the "Little London," where society flourished and colonial ladies wore bonnets of silk. The city was built up from the mud around them, and alligators swam the waters just outside town. It was a society built on utopian ideals, a perfect experiment pitting the intentions of honorable men against unspeakable hardships.

And somehow, out of each new challenge, the city rose again stronger, firmer in its identity than before. This place, too beautiful for even the ruthless General Sherman to burn during his March to the Sea, has birthed innovation and culture that changed the course of a nation. Men whose names echo in history once walked its streets. And those who come to visit today are bound to hear tales and legends of the Hostess City that have been told ten thousand times before.

But what of the countless faces seemingly forgotten, the names that history held in looser grip but whose souls left impressions too deep to disappear? Savannah's hidden history is long and wide, as murky as its coastal river and capricious as the tossing waves that kiss its island shores.

Savannah's Beginning

The Inspiration for a Colony

Perhaps it's best to start at the beginning. To remember how human hearts dreamed up a place where men could be free to dream and live and work, broken from the bonds of class division and hardship.

It was 1729, and England was securely rooted in a culture marred by prejudice, inequality and social unrest. King George II was on the throne, and the Spanish were racing to establish dominance in the New World. Britain had already laid claim to twelve colonies and was working to expand its global footprint.

James Edward Oglethorpe, remembered as the first governor of Georgia, was born in London to a prominent family and enjoyed a comfortable childhood. It would have been easy to stay within rank, to focus on his own affairs and continue to build the wealth and prestige of his family. But James had the heart of an adventurer, and his views on society and culture, justice and the way he believed things should be navigated his decisions, whether thought out or impulsive. After a stint of formal education, a military foray in Austria and a victorious bid for a seat in the House of Parliament, Oglethorpe's attention was drawn to the people.

James Oglethorpe was said to have been idealistic and passionate about issues of social justice. But when his good friend Robert Castell fell on hard times and was thrown into one of London's dreaded debtor's prisons,

General James Oglethorpe.
Courtesy of the New York Public Library.

Oglethorpe's philosophies were called into action. England's debtor's prisons formed a self-destructive system. Those who could not pay their outstanding debts were held to account by being thrown in prison until they could settle the funds against them. Of course, this was almost impossible to accomplish behind prison walls, and so many who found themselves there never made it out. They were dark, depressing places where otherwise upstanding members of society were treated like criminals and subjected to horrible living conditions. If prisoners could afford to at least pay the prison warden, they could, on occasion, arrange for more tolerable living conditions as they strategized their release. But this was a rare occurrence. Most prisoners died of malnourishment, and more still passed away from diseases like smallpox.

Such was the case with Oglethorpe's friend Castell. His unjust death so troubled Oglethorpe that it sparked an idea, a seed of consolation, if not redemption, for those still suffering. Oglethorpe approached King George II with a proposition: a settlement in the Americas, a new colony, meant to add to Britain's wealth and international standing but also to offer an escape to those who otherwise had no hope of working off their debts. Oglethorpe believed that England's poor deserved a chance to reclaim their lives and better themselves and their futures.

The settlement would be a grand experiment of freedom—a place where Oglethorpe decreed there would be a fresh start for those whose lives depended on it. There were nine hundred applicants to travel to this new classless system in the New World. Ironically, there were no recorded debtors chosen for the first voyage; instead, men and women were chosen for the skills they could lend in establishing the new society.

Oglethorpe and his 114 pre-selected shipmates set off from Gravesend, England, and across the Atlantic on the ship *Anne*, landing on the coast of Georgia nearly two months later in February 1733. The voyage was seven weeks long and bitterly cold. The ship's hull offered little warmth or shelter from the winds and unforgiving climate outside. The quarters were cramped, and privacy was nonexistent. Luxuries like bathing were out of the question, and the cuisine consisted of broth, mutton, wine and any sea life they managed to pull from the Atlantic. The only entertainment they enjoyed was Bible reading. In addition to human passengers, sheep, hogs, ducks and other farm life were their constant shipmates. It was an arduous journey.

In a February 10, 1733 letter to the trustees back in England, available in *General Oglethorpe's Georgia*, James Oglethorpe described their arrival in Savannah:

> *I fixed on a healthy situation about ten miles from the sea. The river there forms a half moon, along the South side of which the banks are about 40-foot-high and upon a top a flat which they call a bluff. The plain high ground extends into the country five or six miles and along the river side about a mile. Ships that draw twelve-foot water can ride within ten yards of the bank. Upon the riverside in the center of this plain I have laid out the town. Over against it is an island* [Hutchison Island] *a very rich land fit for pasturage, which I think should be kept for the Trustees cattle. The river is pretty wide, the water is fresh. And from the quay of the town you see its whole course to the sea with the island of Tybee, which forms*

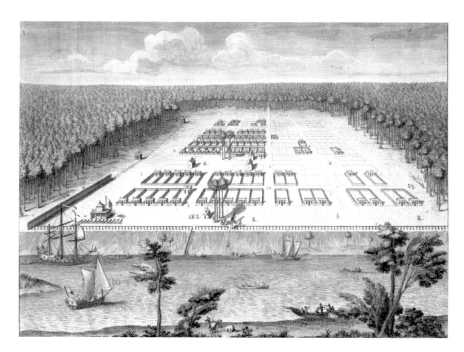

A view of Savannah, 1734. *Courtesy of the New York Public Library.*

the mouth of the river. And the other way you may see the river for about six miles up the country. The landscape is very agreeable, the stream being wide and bordered with high woods on both sides.

Despite the politics, the wealth to be gained and the strategy that inevitably grew from the new colony, it's a wonder to think of how many lives changed course, and what destinies were created, out of Oglethorpe's desire to avenge the death of his dear friend Robert Castell. He left behind a life of ease in favor of a dream come to life. And although things didn't turn out exactly as he planned, he's remembered as the benevolent and successful founder of Savannah.

MARY MUSGROVE

James Oglethorpe's well-laid plans might have quickly met with ruin if it hadn't been for the services of one often-overlooked yet remarkable woman: Mary Musgrove.

She was born "Coosaponakeesa," the daughter of a Creek woman and British settler in today's Coweta, Georgia. The family found their way to South Carolina, where Mary was educated and brought up in the Christian faith. But as she grew, her heritage pulled at her from both directions. She straddled two cultures, speaking both English and the language of the Creeks. Her unique perspective on life and desire to protect her Creek heritage gave her a talent for diplomacy. Entrepreneurial-minded, she began a successful series of trading posts at which she primarily dealt in deerskins.

By the time Mary was thirty-three, she had married her husband, John Musgrove, and the two had moved just outside Yamacraw Bluff to establish a new trading post. By this time, mediation and diplomacy between the Creeks and British was Mary's wheelhouse, and so when she was called on to initiate introductions between Oglethorpe and the Yamacraw chief, Tomochichi, the meeting was already destined for success.

Mary played the vital roles of translator and preliminary peace envoy, ensuring that the settlers established a positive, friendly and equitable relationship from the start. Tomochichi agreed to let Oglethorpe settle where he desired on the bluff, moving his tribe a little upriver. It was an important relationship, as winter was in full swing at the time Oglethorpe arrived and the weather wasn't quite as temperate as they'd expected it to be.

Oglethorpe's interview with Tomochichi. *Courtesy of the New York Public Library.*

With Tomochichi's help, the settlers were able to locate the resources they needed and learn the ins and outs of their new home. Clearly, if it hadn't been for Mary Musgrove's translation skills, the first settlers of Savannah might not have made it through the first winter. Oglethorpe and Tomochichi became fast friends, with Tomochichi accompanying the governor on trips back to England, with Mary's husband, John, acting as translator during the trip.

After the death of her husband in 1735, Mary moved their popular trading post, the Cowpens, closer into town, where it became even more successful. In addition to her deerskin trade, she continued to play a role in translation and diplomacy across the colony.

Mary went on to marry twice more, first to Jacob Matthew, who died only five years into their marriage. A short time after, Mary became the wife of Thomas Boomsworth, a celebrated reverend and a member of the colony's respected upper-middle class. The two of them spent years on missionary trips to the native Creeks, with Mary continuing to lend translation skills to the colonists, who called on her less and less. Once Oglethorpe was recalled to England ten years after establishing the colony, Mary's usefulness in the eyes of the trustees became almost nonexistent.

Years before, in his gratitude to her, Tomochichi had granted Mary lands of her own just outside Savannah. But as her influence with the

British waned, those in power refused to recognize the transaction. Mary fought for years to see her land claims granted, appealing to different courts between England and Georgia. She saw the lands as credits due to her for establishing such important relationships for the early colony. She was eventually awarded St. Catherine's Island by Savannah's governor, Henry Ellis, in 1757. She lived out her life there in peace.

A woman with a spirit far ahead of her time, her heart was too big and loud for the culture that benefited from her bravery. She is remembered now as a savvy businesswoman, a fearless entrepreneur and an integral part of Savannah's survival story.

THE YAMACRAW TRIBE AND TOMOCHICHI

Chief Tomochichi formed the Yamacraw tribe in 1728 after splitting from the lower Creek nation in South Carolina following the Yamasee War of 1715. The Yamasee War was a conflict between South Carolina Native Americans and British traders over disagreements and unrealistic debts placed on the tribes of the region.

Once the war was over, it wasn't long before many Native Americans resumed trading with the British, which, rather understandably, angered Tomochichi. He moved his peace-loving people, numbering about two hundred, south to the edge of the Sabanna River, now known as the Savannah River.

The Yamacraws believed in one god whose spirit inhabited all objects on the earth, which contributed to their nonviolent philosophies. The Yamacraws also possessed highly sophisticated political sensibilities, which, as fate would have it, worked out very well for the arguably naïve Oglethorpe and his settlers.

Oglethorpe was no stranger to the grisly and violent tales of the Yamasee War, and Tomochichi knew that his settlement was small and vulnerable. Each of the men had something to fear of the unknown—something to fear in the other. After mediation under the aid of translator and diplomat Mary Musgrove, Tomochichi and Oglethorpe were, not surprisingly, famously accommodating toward each other. They even became fast friends. As found in the *Political State of Great Britain*, Tomochichi is noted as saying:

> *I was a banished man; I came here poor and helpless to look for good land near the tombs of my ancestors, and the Trustees sent people here; I feared*

you would drive us away, for we were weak and wanted corn; but you confirmed our land to us, gave us food, and instructed our children. We have already thanked you in the strongest words we could find, but words are no return for such favors for good words may be spoke by the deceitful and as by the upright heart. The chief men of all our nation are here to thank you for us; and before them I declare your goodness and that here I design to die, for we all love your people so well that with them we will live and die. We do not know good from evil, but desire to be instructed and guided by you that we may do well with and numbered amongst the children of the Trustees.

It's important to keep in mind that Tomochichi was anything but a pushover. He was constantly strategizing how best to position his small tribe against the influx of more settlers. He saw how an emphasis on peace and collaboration could benefit both peoples well. He had strong feelings about introducing his people to the Christian faith and furthering a European-based education—all with an eye toward upward mobility in the new reality.

On August 1, 1734, Tomochichi traveled to Europe with Oglethorpe and met King George II at Kensington Palace, establishing a treaty called the "Articles of Friendship and Commerce," officially agreeing to Savannah's establishment on Yamacraw Bluff. He was also instrumental in establishing the territory lines between Georgia and Florida. He died content and well remembered on October 5, 1739, far into his late nineties.

Upon his death, Tomochichi was fondly remembered by Savannah's people, and his remains were buried in the center of what then was called Percival Square, marked by a traditional stone-covered burial mound. Tomochichi's grave remained undisturbed until 1883. When William Washington Gordon, the founder of the Central of Georgia Railroad Company and grandfather of Juliette Gordon Low, passed away in 1842, the City of Savannah decided to erect a grand memorial in the center of Wright Square in his honor, leveling Tomochichi's memorial. However, Gordon's daughter-in-law, Nellie, ordered a boulder of granite moved from Stone Mountain to the square and stationed adjacent to the original grave site in honor of the noble chief.

His remains still rest today in the center of Savannah's Wright Square.

THE GEORGIA TRUSTEES

Trustees were members of British Parliament entrusted with governing colonies from Britain, allowing for an experimental period to see if the proposed colony would work. Trustees received no special incentives or considerations for their time or commitment to their projects, which was why Oglethorpe lived an incredibly modest lifestyle during his decade-long tenure in Savannah. His motto was *Non sibi sed aliis* ("Not for self, but for others"), and he lived the phrase to the fullest, ever demonstrating his humanitarian mindset.

While Oglethorpe is often credited as Georgia's first governor, he technically would not have been able to hold office as one of Georgia's original twenty-one trustees. The symbolic honor has stood the test of time all the same.

LIFE IN EARLY SAVANNAH

Starting out, of course, the settlement of Savannah was very primitive. In fact, James Oglethorpe resided in little more than a tent for the duration of time he spent in there. But as rough as the original encampment was, the plan for construction and growth was incredibly organized. Savannah is credited for being America's first planned city, meaning there was a very distinct plan behind how and why the parameters of town were first established.

Inspired by a military mindset, Oglethorpe enacted a Ward System, meaning that a series of town squares were intended first and foremost as gathering places for troops, as well as high-functioning community centers. The positioning of Oglethorpe's original squares ensured that if Savannah were invaded, the colonists could gather troops, such as they were, to defend the city, square by square.

There were four original squares: Johnson, Wright, Telfair and Ellis Square. Each square had a total of forty homes, a church and a government meeting place to represent the ward. Each family was granted five acres of land on the edge of Savannah for personal gardening and forty-five more aces beyond that to cultivate agriculture for market. Oglethorpe believed that fifty acres and a home was sufficient to create a good life—the conditions being that families would work their own land and that none of what had been given could be sold for at least three years.

Colonial life in Savannah was not glamorous by any stretch of the imagination. There were few comforts to be found beyond the warmth of an evening fire or the appreciation of wide-open, beautiful adventure. Settlers' homes were mean cabins, most often constructed in a hurry, and they afforded little more than shade from the hot Georgia sun. The squares were very exposed to the elements and devoid of trees, as it made them easier to defend in the case of an attack. Spanish-occupied Florida sat very near to the south, and the underlying tension over potential invasion was constant. All able-bodied men were expected to learn how to wield a sword, a musket and a bayonet.

Georgia's settlers needed access to the basic necessities of life while they helped to build the city and established new homes from the ground up. They relied on the Trustees Store, an establishment funded with supplies for the settlers that they could access at very little cost for the first year of the colony. James Oglethorpe was the go-to authority until he took a brief trip back to England in March 1734 to personally address the Georgia Trustees on the colony's progress. The man Oglethorpe had appointed as the store shopkeeper, Thomas Causton, was left briefly in charge—for as much as that meant at the time. Causton was accused of abuse of power because he lorded his newfound authority over the people and tried to control who could have what supplies from the Trustees Store, manipulating them to do his will. He ran the colony for his personal gain, illegally transporting alcohol, taking advantage of trustees' servants, embezzling money and falsifying official statements. Desperate for Oglethorpe's return, the settlers petitioned the trustees to remove Causton.

Upon Oglethorpe's return, it was apparent that one of his greatest challenges was trusting people who had never been in leadership roles before to take on these new responsibilities. Although he'd received more than three hundred individual grievances from the people, he levied no official punishment over Causton.

Despite such constant dramas of flailing governance, daily life was focused primarily on agriculture, with an eye always toward progress and attracting new settlers to join the colony. Charleston sat just up the coast, and having been established sixty-six years earlier, it was markedly more attractive. It took patience and grit to ride out the dawning of a new settlement. Gnats, mosquitoes and river rats proved to be constant companions. The heat and humidity of the summer took a toll, and the wet spring season ensured that the streets passed for little more than overgrown mud pies.

But ever passionate, Savannah had something going for it that Charleston did not: the drive of James Oglethorpe. His ideals for his time were inspired. Whether out of kindred philosophies or simply the desire for the freedom that comes with a fresh start, men and women quite literally staked their lives on seeing Oglethorpe's vision for Savannah come to fruition. He had four laws in particular that made Savannah unique:

- No LAWYERS: Oglethorpe said that a lawyer's job is to represent opposing sides on an issue, and the last thing he wanted were people fighting.
- No HARD LIQUOR: Oglethorpe especially didn't like rum, thinking that it corrupted the mind. However, beer and wine were acceptable, as they were afraid to drink the water.
- No ROMAN CATHOLICS: This was due, of course, to the ongoing war against the Spanish.
- No SLAVERY: Oglethorpe stated, "If our motto is not for ourselves, but for others, it defeats our whole purpose of being here to have slaves."

THE ST. ANDREW'S SOCIETY, THE HIGHLANDER'S NEW INVERNESS AND THE MALCONTENTS

The Scottish were counted among the earliest of Savannah's settlers, although the Lowlanders and Highlanders tended to side on social topics with varying degrees of exuberance.

Named for the patron saint of Scotland, the St. Andrew's Society was established in 1737 in Savannah, making it the first society of its kind established in the Georgia colony. The establishment was in line with other branches of the Scottish society, like the one begun in Charleston in 1729, and focused on charity and relief for struggling Scottish settlers, as well as promoting Scottish interests within the New World.

Savannah's original Highlanders—177 men, women and children—left Inverness, Scotland, in October 1735 and arrived in Savannah in January 1736. In accordance with Oglethorpe's military mindset, the mighty Scottish were immediately recruited to settle the area known as New Inverness, later called Darian, Georgia. Oglethorpe was known to show a particular affinity toward the Highlanders, enlisting their battle-trained aid against the Spanish at his forts in Darian and St. Simons Island. They defended the forts with their traditional shields and broadswords and were free to sport their kilts and bonnets as they saw fit.

In 1740, Oglethorpe led the Highlanders in a failed attack against the Spanish-held St. Augustine. He lost sixty-eight men in the battle, which ended in retreat. The Spanish retaliated with an attack against St. Simons's Fort Frederica in the Battle of Gully Hole Creek in June 1742. Oglethorpe and the Highlanders held off the Spanish and won the battle.

The Battle of Bloody Marsh took place on the same day, also on St. Simons Island; the Highlanders, on their own, were able to push the Spanish back into Florida for good. The battle was named in celebration of the purported Spanish blood–soaked marshes, although only seven Spanish soldiers were actually killed. Oglethorpe's preference for Highlander company brought attention to the Jacobite-leaning tendencies of his family and, on occasion, called his own British loyalties into question.

Not everyone agreed with Oglethorpe's four laws of prohibition (no lawyers, no Roman Catholics, no liquor and no slaves). Unlike Oglethorpe's Highlanders on the southerly edge of the colony, Savannah's Lowlander population had come with the intention of social freedom and the expansion of wealth. They arrived in about 1735, equipped with money and resources to spare. In particular, they believed that the outlawing of liquor was intolerable and unreasonable. They frequented the local taverns for beer and graced the colony with what would have been considered uncouth revelry and displays of copious unbridled passions. While the Highlanders championed Oglethorpe's feelings on freedom for all, the Lowlanders chafed against antislavery laws, as well as restrictions on the ownership of land acres.

The Lowlanders became known as the "Malcontents," and they petitioned the trustees in England for amendments to Oglethorpe's strict policies. They were denied. The Malcontents continued to protest, arguing that if the colony didn't loosen regulations, it would fail. They continued to make life in the colony a colorful display of boisterous protest until they finally left for Charleston in 1740.

In line with the Malcontents' prediction, the exodus became a trend among the settlers, one that ultimately threatened the strength of the population Oglethorpe's idyllic settlement required.

WOMEN AND MARRIAGE IN COLONIAL SAVANNAH

When it came to marriage in early Savannah, it was less about romance and more about survival. Women were understood to be integral members of the new society from the very beginning, making up a sizable portion of the first 114 settlers who first arrived with James Oglethorpe in 1733.

In the beginning, the idea of contractual marriages for advancement fell by the wayside, and love at the start of a marriage would have been considered a fortunate accident. Marriage centered solely on survival and the advancement of the homefront.

Despite the lack of romantic sensibilities, women were actually prioritized and well taken care of in the early colony; a special stipend was even provided for the payment and welfare of a hired midwife who could be on hand for all births, as well as tend to the minor medical needs of women and other citizens as time allowed.

In the beginning, women were not entitled to inherit the lands of their husbands or father, which initially served to make sure that there was a man on every plot of land capable of defense. Eventually, the rule was overturned, and women slowly gained more control of their destinies within the colony.

Divorce was a topic completely out of the question, which made life for some women rather unbearable. Most women were forced to marry out of necessity, especially if they had been recently widowed. There wasn't always time to wait for a man who made the perfect match. A roof over their heads, security for any children they might have and safety in the Lowcountry wilds were priorities. Some women, however, found their marriages too hard to bear and opted to escape by ship or by perilous land journeys to other neighboring colonies for a chance at a fresh start.

THE TRUSTEES GARDEN

One of Oglethorpe's first orders of business was to try to figure out what would grow in Savannah. He set his eyes on a ten-acre plot of land on the edge of the settlement that he called the Trustees Garden. He had botanists sent to South America and the West Indies to collect plants and seeds and bring them back to Savannah.

His greatest hope was that mulberry trees would grow, as he wanted the colony to produce highly profitable silks. This wasn't the case, of course.

The mulberry trees struggled in the humid, intemperate southern climate, only ever producing enough silk to make one dress, which was gifted to Queen Caroline.

It was a new colony, and the gardens were a grand experiment. Cotton, flax, hemp, rice and other crops were grown there. The hopes that Savannah would be an agricultural mecca—and, in turn, grow the wealth of the British empire—was at the forefront of the founders' minds. But lack of knowledgeable farmers and the coastal weather made for a hard go of it. The experimental gardens were eventually decommissioned and assimilated into bordering residential areas by the mid-1750s.

HURRAY HUSSARS

Near the corner of today's Liberty and Bull Streets stands an odd yet charming little building. Visitors pass by it often, catching their reflections in the tall glass windows and taking a moment to study the terra-cotta façade that looks like something out of Arabia. However, the building signifies one of Savannah's most noble hidden histories, a treasured city relic ever alluding to the bravery of men entrusted with one mission: protect Georgia from its enemies, always.

In 1736, founder James Oglethorpe established the Georgia Hussars, elite mounted rangers, at the time meant to protect the Georgian colony from the threat of Spanish invasion from Florida. Highly skilled, their job was to protect the borders at any cost. In one of their greatest shows of strength, they defended Georgia in the Battle of Bloody Marsh in 1742, ultimately helping to establish a definitive Florida/Georgia line.

The Hussars risked death during the doomed Siege of Savannah in 1779, going on to fight in the Civil War, the world wars, the Vietnam War and every American-involved war since, remaining cavalry-mounted until 1944.

The unassuming building that stands in Historic Savannah now was built in 1897 as a market space to fund the Hussars' ongoing defense efforts. Today, it's a popular upscale bar, committed to preserving the site's unique history. Remarkably, the Hussars are still an active division of the Georgia National Guard today.

FORT HALIFAX, FORT WAYNE—ALL THE SAME

Just down a grassy knoll from the Trustees Garden, a brick wall hugs the edge of the hill. Easily overlooked, this is an important feature in Savannah's history, the scene of intrigue and violence over the years.

The wall belonged to the original Fort Halifax. Savannah lies forty-two feet above the Savannah River on the north end, naturally protected by its positioning on Yamacraw Bluff. But Oglethorpe knew the importance of securing Savannah's east side from an attack by the Spanish. He established the fort, lining it with cannons to protect the edge of the city.

Over the years, improvements were made to the structure, yet the more sophisticated and reinforced Fort Halifax wasn't called on until the Revolutionary War. It proved more useful to the British, though, who called it Fort Prevost and used it against its own people once they'd taken the city. They reinforced the fort themselves, making adjustments and improvements over the four years they occupied it. Once the colonists had regained Savannah, they renamed the site Fort Wayne, after a prominent Revolutionary general.

Savannah and its economy grew quickly following the Revolution. Newer forts, including Fort Jackson, just east of the city, proved to be more advanced. It wasn't long before Fort Wayne was assimilated into the city, no longer useful as a working fortification.

A JEWISH DOCTOR AND A SYNAGOGUE

Savannah's Jewish heritage is a little-shared highlight that led to a big legacy.

It was a desperate bid for a fresh start. The ship *William and Sarah* had set off from England only weeks after Oglethorpe's ship, *Anne*, and yet the group of forty-two Jewish settlers traveled for five months, arriving first in North Carolina and then finding their way south, where their distressed ship landed on the coast of Oglethorpe's Georgia.

The group was predominately Portuguese, their previous tenure in England having lasted about a decade before the prejudices against them there set them in search of a new home yet again. It just so happened that a doctor, Samuel Nunes, was aboard. When the group arrived, they found Savannah's colonial settlers suffering from an intestinal disease that had taken the life of Savannah's first doctor a short time before.

Mickve Israel Synagogue. *Courtesy of the Jeff Bush Photography Collection.*

Doctor Nunes was able to treat and save the lives of many of Savannah's early residents, and out of gratitude, General Oglethorpe, against the wishes of the trustees, welcomed the Jewish families to stay and settle. As found on the Jewish Virtual Library website (www.jewishvirtuallibrary.org), the ensuing congregation was the first to receive a letter of blessing from President George Washington in 1790:

May the same wonder-working Deity, who long since delivering the Hebrews from their Egyptian Oppressors planted them in the promised land—whose providential agency has lately been conspicuous in establishing these United States as an independent nation—still continue to water them with the dews of Heaven and to make the inhabitants of every denomination participate in the temporal and spiritual blessings of that people whose God is Jehovah.

The culture took root and led to the architecture of Savannah's Mickve Israel, a stunning, Gothic Revival cathedral-style synagogue completed in 1878. It still houses the original Torah brought over in 1733 and attracts visitors by the thousands.

IRISH ASHORE

Most people have heard of Savannah's St. Patrick's Day Parade celebrations, but not many Savannah locals know how the Irish came to be in Savannah in the first place.

It was a shipwreck that landed the first Irish settlers on Savannah's shores. Although the colony at first prohibited Catholicism (due to the ongoing war with the Spanish to the south), Oglethorpe was not the kind of governor who could turn away a huddled mass of terrified survivors.

The ship had been filled with indentured servants on their way to New England when a storm turned them off course and toward the coast of Georgia. Of the well over one hundred passengers, there were only forty survivors: six women and thirty-four men. The survivors were starving, injured, sick and desperate not to return to the ocean.

Oglethorpe bought their contracts for £5 per servant from their previously assigned families to the north, totaling a personal cost of £200, a sum that would equal $51,800 in today's values. He reissued them as

Factor's Walk.
*Courtesy of the Jeff
Bush Photography
Collection.*

indentured servants to plantation owners in Savannah, recouping his costs
and circumventing his own antislavery law in a unique way.

It was a boon for the Irish, as the northern cities were often a death
sentence due to working conditions. Oglethorpe had just handed them an
opportunity and hope for the future. This was a place where freedom could
actually come true, where they would be able to work and establish lands
and homes for themselves. A fresh start. A new beginning. And all in line
with the governor's original intent for the city.

Despite the opportunities, the Irish were still indentured servants (and
Catholic to boot) and were treated like second-class citizens for years to
come. It was the potato famine between 1830 and 1860 that saw 2,200
Irish immigrate to Savannah's shores as relatives established lives and
wrote to family members across the ocean to come and join them in the
land of opportunity.

for manning Factor's Walk along the Savannah River, the Irish loaded cotton bales onto ships and barges, while others were widely responsible for contributing to the infrastructure of the growing city. Savannah's Irish heritage is a proud and vibrant one that still inspires recognition and celebration today.

The Scandal of John Wesley and Sophia Hopkey

John Wesley was the founder of the Methodist Church, beginning at Lincoln College in Oxford, England. His younger brother, Charles, started a religious group that met every day for prayer and lessons. The methodology was very strict, and so they became known as Methodists.

Oglethorpe requested John Wesley to come to Savannah as head minister, as he was known as someone very strict and regimented in his ways. Wesley traveled to Savannah with his brother, Charles, as well as John Whitfield, who would later go on to found the Bethesda Orphanage, America's first for children. Scandal wouldn't be far behind, and her name was Sophia Hopkey.

Wesley arrived in February 1736, only three years into the life of the colony. Wesley looked at the move not only as a way to lead his own congregation but also as a mission to convert Native Americans to the Christian faith.

Wesley met Sophia fresh off the boat and paid her special attention that could only be presumed as attraction, but Wesley was conflicted. He agreed to teach her French, which of course would have meant quite a bit of time spent together. But Wesley believed that his primary calling was his role with the church.

Sophia eventually married another man, William Williamson. Wesley became jealous and standoffish and even went so far as to deny Hopkey communion at church, saying that she had fallen from the faith, leaving Hopkey's virtue in question. Sophia's husband sued John Wesley for £1,000 in sterling for the defamation. The chief magistrate of the trial was none other than Thomas Causton, the widely disliked guardian of the colony in Oglethorpe's absence.

Wesley's motion had backfired. The scandal grew until the matter ended in mistrial, and Wesley was eventually asked to leave Savannah. He returned to England just shy of two years after his arrival, but with the credit of founding American Methodism to his name.

WORMSLOE PLANTATION

Visitors to Savannah traditionally make a trip to the site of Wormsloe Plantation, eager to take a photo of the iconic oak-shrouded lane just behind its front gates. But few learn the history of the plantation ruins that remain. Wormsloe Plantation is situated on the Isle of Hope right outside downtown Savannah. Native American tribes had lived there for centuries—specifically the Yamacraw—by the time Oglethorpe and his settlers arrived on the shores of Georgia in 1733.

In 1736, Noble Jones, one of the original trustees, asked for a grant of five hundred acres on the isle. He was a carpenter upon arrival but soon after became a doctor, a successful businessman and a contributor to Savannah's establishment. Wormsloe Plantation, said to be named after his home in England, became a fortification and lookout for enemy Spanish troops stationed in Florida. The home was made of tabby, a concrete made from oyster shells and lyme. Eight-foot walls surrounded the architectural wonder.

Coming from the well, Wormsloe Plantation. *Courtesy of the New York Public Library.*

Noble Jones initially utilized indentured servants to assist with crops and running the plantation, but once slavery was established in Savannah in 1751, his plantation flourished with crops of corn and rice. Noble died just before the Revolutionary War in 1775, leaving Wormsloe to his daughter, Mary Jones Bulloch.

It's believed that pirates used the land of Wormsloe Plantation for hiding buried treasure, leading to more than a few unsuccessful treasure hunts. And in times of yellow fever outbreak, Savannah residents were known at one time to have flocked behind the high walls of the plantation.

The grounds of Wormsloe Plantation are among Savannah's most picturesque and hallowed treasures. The descendants of Noble Jones still manage the grounds today.

THE GREAT DIVIDE: OGLETHORPE VERSUS SAVANNAH

As the years passed, and despite any initial bravado, a mass of settlers eventually left Georgia for an easier go of it in Charleston, leaving dangerous few people behind to maintain the colony. In November 1737, William Stephens arrived in Savannah, armed with political smarts and plenty of gumption.

Land tenure was a big debate at the time, as was growing tension around Oglethorpe's strict rules, specifically when it came to the prohibition of rum and slavery. Charleston was flourishing just to the north, and many Savannahians believed that Oglethorpe's rules were holding the colony back.

Stephens actually agreed with Oglethorpe's views on slavery and rum, but he could see the issues with land trusts brewing. The land trusts decreed that only men could inherit land, which meant that widows and female orphans had no foothold in society and no way to continue the legacies in which they'd been so long involved. The counterargument was that if women were left the land, they might not be able to defend it properly against attack or manage it with the sensibilities of men.

But as the colony grew, the need for every landholding citizen to be male made less and less sense. Stephens understood this and made his opinions known. Because Oglethorpe was spending so much time traveling between Savannah and London, out negotiating trade agreements with Native Americans and defending Georgia from its enemies, he needed someone to manage Savannah's daily duties. He chose William Stephens.

With William Stephens's increasing daily involvement in Savannah's finances, daily affairs and management, his fellow citizens' trust in him grew, resulting in the catalyst of opposition between Stephens and Oglethorpe that divided Savannah. Stephens eventually took control of Frederica, the area the colonists called the "north end" of the city by the river; the rest of the south end was called Savannah, which became Oglethorpe's domain.

Faced with the slow deconstruction of the dream he'd chased, and after a growing disenchantment among the settlers toward his hard-and-fast rules of prohibition, James Oglethorpe himself left the New World for England on July 23, 1743, and never returned.

To the surprise of most, the colony didn't go under without the leadership of its dauntless founder, although trade relations with Native Americans were gravely affected, securing Savannah in economic turmoil that would follow it up to the Revolution. In James Oglethorpe's absence, the trustees granted William Stephens leadership of Georgia. He remained president of the struggling colony until 1751.

With new leadership came new regulation.

ROYAL SAVANNAH

After years of destitute turmoil and the disillusionment of any and all grand beginnings, Georgia ceased to be under trustee rule and transitioned to a royal province in 1755. The first lawyers were admitted into Georgia in 1758 and commenced duties by writing the Georgia Slave Code, although slavery had technically crept into Savannah shortly after the death of William Stephens. The change increased land cultivation and the formation of plantations, sparking renewed exports to Europe.

LITTLE LONDON

The way landowners got around Oglethorpe's antislavery regulation was reliant on "adventurers," groups that brought indentured servants to Georgia in droves. The patrons would pay for their passage to the New World in exchange for the indentured servants working for them until their debts were paid off. It was a convenient way to bring on moderately priced labor, but it still wasn't enough to assuage the colony's thirst for growth.

After Oglethorpe's departure, pressure grew to allow slavery. South Carolina had a thriving economy, rich with rice and cotton exports. Georgia was a mud pit where no one wanted to live. Leadership eventually conceded to accept slavery, and less than a decade later, Savannah was called "Little London." It was then common to walk down the streets greeting women in silk bonnets, fine dresses and expensive parasols. Gentlemen dressed in suits as they entered libraries or taverns. An education system was now in place.

By 1760, the population of Georgia had grown to 6,000, including 3,500 slaves. Nearly one slave for every two people, the foundation of this new way of life coming at the hands of Senegal Africans. Georgia's first bale of cotton reached Liverpool in 1764, beginning the colony's rise to a major player in cotton exchange.

Ironically, it was deer hide that established Savannah as an economic powerhouse from 1764 to 1773. Most of the hides came through inland Georgia, down the Savannah River and were eventually exported to Europe.

THE FIRST ROYAL GOVERNOR JOHN REYNOLDS AND THE ALMOST CITY OF HARDWICKE

British naval captain John Reynolds became the first royal governor of Georgia in October 1754. He was an unenthusiastic governor, particularly fixated on his drop in salary rather than on his technical rise in station, and made it clear at every turn he would take the first appealing situation he could find to get out of the fledgling colony.

John Reynolds was discontent with the location of Savannah as Georgia's capital. He felt that the city, positioned where it was on a high bluff above the water, made for difficult access and placed undo stress on the efforts for the colony's growth.

As found in *The History of Georgia: Aboriginal and Colonial Epochs*, Reynolds favored what he called the city of Hardwicke to become the new capital city, which would be where the city of Georgetown sits today, a half-hour automobile ride south of Savannah. "[I]t has a charming situation," he said of his chosen location, "the winding of the river, making it a peninsula. And it is the only fit place for the capitol."

The idea earned high opposition with Savannah's wealthy landowners and never received the financial backing it needed to get off the ground. Ultimately, Governor Reynolds was a widely disliked leader, the epitome of a loose cannon. The people of Savannah were widely disappointed that Reynolds wasn't more invested in and passionate about the colony and its future. Noble Jones and James Habersham were among the most vocally unhappy and pressed England for a change in command. For the sake of the colony, he was recalled to England in 1757.

THE ORIGINAL PIRATE'S HOUSE

The Pirate's House was originally constructed in 1734, at first functioning as the garden house for Oglethorpe's Trustees Garden. An addition came in 1753, when it was established as an inn and pub for seafarers. Pirates from as far as Asia and the Caribbean frequented the inn. In fact, Robert Louis Stephenson included the establishment in his novel *Treasure Island*. Countless pirates frequented the inn, including the infamous Anne Bonny, known to be one of the fiercest pirates to sail the Caribbean. She was famous for declaring to her enemies, "If you had fought like a man, you needn't be hanged like a dog."

But it's what lies hidden beneath the Pirate's House that is most fascinating. A series of tunnels runs from the basement level, carved through to what was historically the bluffs of the Savannah River. There are many theories as to the use of the tunnels, including bootlegging and smuggling. Pirates would commandeer new recruits from inside the inn, usually young men who'd had too much to drink. They'd carry them through the tunnels and out to

The Pirate's House. *Courtesy of the Jeff Bush Photography Collection.*

the ships waiting down the river outside. Once the men woke up the next morning, the ships would already be far out to sea. Famously, the captives were told, "You can join the crew, or you're free to swim home."

Today, the old Trustees Garden House portion of the Pirate's House stands as the oldest building in Georgia.

THE SECOND ROYAL GOVERNOR, HENRY ELLIS

The vacancy left by Governor John Reynolds made way for Savannah's second royal governor, Henry Ellis, the namesake of Savannah's downtown city market Ellis Square. Henry Ellis was a sailor, dealing in the slave trade during the early 1750s. His work as governor was markedly more appealing to Savannah's population. Ellis was particularly apt at dealing with the Native American tribes in the region, his unscrupulous past having prepared him for intercultural negotiations. Savannah's trade economy boomed under Ellis's influence.

Henry Ellis is credited as establishing Georgia's first true and organized government and economy. Somehow he managed to create order within the chaos that Savannah had fallen under—teaching the people how to self-govern and laying the groundwork for future success in spheres like established county parishes, city budgets, tax structure and an advanced credit system. Despite his past in the slave trade, Ellis pushed for regulation that would make slaves free citizens upon turning thirty. His efforts were unanimously shot down.

His numerous accomplishments earned Ellis the unofficial title of "Savannah's second founder." While he was a well-liked and successful governor, Ellis only held the station for three years, as poor health forced him back to England.

SAVANNAH'S FIRST NEWSPAPER

Savannah's first newspaper was the *Georgia Gazette*. The paper was printed by James Johnston, who was also appointed to print the laws of the colony in 1762 by the Provincial Assembly. It was an honor to be granted the task, and as such, Johnston was referred to as the "Royal Printer."

Johnston's original paper usually ran only four pages long and reported on the news of the colony. The original press stood where Savannah's famous Marshall House stands today. The *Gazette of the State of Georgia*, as it came to be named after the Revolutionary War, ran its last edition in 1802.

Johnston was one of the first journalists in American history to be known to cover both sides of the Revolutionary War from an impartial and fair standpoint. He was highly regarded as a true and honest journalist. He maintained his balanced method of coverage until his death at seventy years old on October 4, 1808.

THE ROYAL GOVERNOR JAMES WRIGHT: WITNESS TO A REVOLUTION

After a brief interlude under the tutelage of Governor Ellis, James Wright formally took the position of Savannah's third and final royal governor in 1760.

James Wright was remarkably good at the job. A passionately loyal British subject, he took ownership over Savannah and its success with the dedication of Oglethorpe and Ellis. The assemblies managing the city had been well educated by Ellis, and so Wright started his tenure with a marked advantage over his predecessors. Wright played a large role in negotiating land deals with the Cherokees in exchange for debt forgiveness, expanding Britain's landholdings substantially.

However, Governor Wright would not be without his enemies. The first grumblings of revolution had only just begun in 1765 with the arrival of the Stamp Act and persisted throughout the latter part of his governance. The Savannah-based Liberty Boys were a particular opposition, at one point hanging Wright in effigy to the cheering of crowds outside the Governor's Mansion.

When a group of British warships stopped by Savannah in January 1776, Wright was smuggled across Bonaventure Plantation and out of the colony. He returned for a short time to England before coming back to govern the British-held Savannah in 1779 and stood his ground until 1782, when the British relinquished Georgia.

REVOLUTIONARY SAVANNAH

From the next generation, held under looser rule, who've watched the Yamacraws and the Creeks and the children of their own time run free in a world where a lofty king has never set foot, an idea emerges—a sentiment that maybe, just maybe, they could sail this ship on their own. That to be all but forgotten, ruled by a cool, uninvested parliament, was not a necessity but an option—and their choice was no.

THE STAMP ACT: AN ACCIDENTAL WAR CRY

Once the British took over Florida following the French and Indian War in 1763, their national debt doubled, and the cost of employing British soldiers on American soil was staggering. The solution? Tax the colonies. After what was felt to be a frivolous Sugar Act levied in 1764, the Stamp Act was imposed fresh on its heels in 1765, the second of many opposed tax declarations on the colonists.

The specifics of the Stamp Act demanded that many necessary papers, including legal documents, and even papers as trivial as game cards had to be specially sourced from particular "stamped" paper from Britain and paid for strictly in British currency. This, of course, caused financial and operational headaches across the colonies and successfully riled up sensibilities in Savannah, with opponents famously claiming "taxation without representation."

It wasn't long before Savannah was split between Loyalists to the Crown and revolutionaries, angry and thirsty for change. The Loyalists—or Tories, as they were called—comprised mostly older generations, often the wealthy who banked off trade agreements with England. Tories also regularly received land from England in order to expand their plantations, so despite the increase in taxes, it was in their own best interests financially to maintain the status quo. But the younger generation was more in favor of separation. There was a clear divide not only on the streets of Savannah but also within its homes.

Imagine a small city divided—a colony destined for war.

JAMES HABERSHAM AND HIS SONS OF LIBERTY

It's hard to come to Savannah without noticing the cargo ships, laden with goods moving in and out of Savannah's port down the Savannah River. Not many know that the original shipping merchant of the Hostess City was none other than James Habersham, the man who first established the transatlantic trading of goods going from Savannah to England, constructing ships for the sole purpose of exports.

The idea came about in an effort to aid the children of Bethesda Orphanage, an institution he supported and helped to manage. There was often a shortage of supplies for the children, so Habersham saw the exporting and importing of goods into the city as a direct line for Bethesda, which had just been founded by George Whitfield in 1740, securing it as the oldest childcare institution in the United States.

By 1744, Habersham's transatlantic trips had begun not only supporting the orphanage but also setting James apart as a master of industry. Perhaps surprisingly, he was also a major advocate for slavery, at the forefront of seeing it come to pass in Georgia in 1751; he grew rice, Georgia's predominate export at the time, on his plantation of fifteen thousand acres.

A British supporter based mainly on his economic standing, he was very loyal to the king. So, imagine the surprise when James's three sons—John, Joseph and James Habersham Jr.—made it clear they were proud supporters of the Revolution. While their father's wealth and enterprise had secured them as men of means and opportunity on their own, they didn't see eye to eye with their father on the need for continued support and trade with the British. It's a classic example of what occurred all across the colony.

Left: James Habersham. *Courtesy of the New York Public Library.*

Right: Major John Habersham. *Courtesy of the New York Public Library.*

Immediate families were separated straight down the middle, pitting brother against brother and sons against fathers in very real life-and-death scenarios.

Each of Habersham's sons went on to contribute greatly to the war efforts in various ways. But first came the days they called themselves the "Liberty Boys."

TONDEE'S TAVERN AND THE SONS OF LIBERTY

Another tax levied, and the first whispers of revolution were on the southern wind. It was a time of extreme tension in Savannah, boiled down mainly to economics clashing with loyalties.

Tondee's Tavern, owned by Peter Tondee, was a place of gathering for all in Savannah and the city's main drinking tavern, but it was also a place for community gatherings where children played freely and decisions were made. The original Tondee's Tavern would have been located at the corner of today's Broughton and Whitaker Streets. On July 20, 1774, Noble Wimberly Jones, Archibald Bullock (who became Georgia's first independent

Tondee's Tavern. *Courtesy of the Jeff Bush Photography Collection.*

governor), John Houston and George Walton assembled a meeting at Tondee's to discuss taxation and the Liberty Boys were born—a band of revolutionaries responsible for stirring the pot in Savannah.

Before there was the Boston Tea Party, there was the Liberty Boys. In 1775, they caused quite a stir in Savannah when they rolled twenty-one cannons down a bluff, erected a Liberty Poll in Johnson Square, tarred and feathered Loyalist John Hopkins—parading him down the street—and even hung Royal Governor Wright in effigy.

The Liberty Boys were the pre-Revolutionary shakers of Savannah, truly stirring things up a full decade before the Declaration of Independence was ever signed.

LACHLAN MCINTOSH AND BUTTON GWINNETT: RIVALS AT WAR

Lachlan McIntosh was directly descended from the original Scottish settlers who came to Savannah in 1736. He was raised at Bethesda Orphanage after the death of his father. A colonel in the Georgia militia in 1776, he commanded the first Georgia regiment, organizing the defense of Savannah from the British.

Button Gwinnett was a member of the Liberty Boys and one of McIntosh's most vehement rivals. He wrote the first original draft of Georgia's first state constitution and was a signer of the Declaration of Independence. Although both McIntosh and Gwinnett were members of the Georgia Assembly, they were political opponents, with McIntosh very involved in the field, while Gwinnett directed most of his initiatives from the assembly.

In 1777, Button Gwinnett was assigned the commander in chief of Georgia's military, making him officially McIntosh's superior. Button ordered McIntosh to go to east Florida, and the resulting battle against the British failed, raising tensions between them even higher.

Gwinnett was running for governor at this time, and Lachlan openly supported Gwinnett's opponent, calling Gwinnet "a scoundrel and lying rascal." Gwinnett, incensed, challenged McIntosh to a duel. At the time, to deny a challenge to duel meant you were seen as a coward. To deny, McIntosh would have been disgraced, especially in front of his troops. He had no choice.

Wayne Lynch in the *Journal of the American Revolution* reported that on May 16, 1777, the two assembled on Governor Wright's pasture, just north of Savannah, along with their seconds. They counted out ten paces. Thereafter, Button said, "Two more." Twelve paces.

Their seconds asked them, "Would you like to turn your back to each other?"

Lachlan responded, "By no means, let us see what we are about."

Both men simultaneously fired; each of them was hit in the leg. The seconds asked them if they wanted to take another shot. Both men demured, meeting in the middle to shake hands, as was honorable.

Lachlan McIntosh. *Courtesy of the New York Public Library.*

Three days later, on May 19, Button Gwinnett succumbed to his wounds and passed away. Lynch writes that Lyman Hall, who was his closest friend and fellow signer of the Declaration of Independence, said, "Oh, Liberty! Why do you suffer so many of your faithful sons, your warmest votaries to fall at your shrine! Alas, my friend! My friend!"

Lachlan McIntosh went on to live, although his reputation was forever wounded. He died in Savannah on February 20, 1806. His home, which also served as George Washington's Savannah headquarters in 1791, still stands today on the corner of Drayton Street and Oglethorpe Avenue.

BUTTON GWINNETT'S SIGNATURE

Button Gwinnett isn't a name that many Americans are likely to remember from history class. It might be surprising to learn that his signature is considered by some to be the most valuable of anyone in American history— more valuable than the signature of any U.S. president, Dr. Martin Luther King Jr., Albert Einstein or any celebrity.

Button is rather accidentally notable for being a last-minute replacement for the meetings of delegates tasked with planning the Declaration of Independence in Philadelphia, along with Lyman Hall and George Walton.

In fact, Button didn't sign the Declaration of Independence officially until August 2, 1776.

There are only fifty-one known examples of Button's signature, ten of them in private hands. Today, a single copy of Button Gwinnett's signature is worth between $500,000 to $1 million.

Casimir Pulaski

Chances are you've heard the name of Pulaski. Monuments and roads, holidays even, are named in honor of the Polish general. But not many know the story behind the brave patriot.

In the 1770s, Casimir Pulaski achieved grand success in defending his home country of Poland as it fought for its own freedom. As found in Jack Manning's "Pulaski Is Born" article, Benjamin Franklin wrote of Pulaski, "Count Pulaski of Poland, an officer famous throughout Europe for his bravery and conduct in defense of the liberties of his country against the three great invading powers of Russia, Austria, and Prussia…may be highly useful to our service."

Noting that Casimir was a success at going after a giant of an opponent for his own country's freedom, Franklin believed that he could help America win its freedom against the giant force of the British.

Upon arrival in 1777, as noted in Congressional records, Casimir wrote to General George Washington, "I came here, where freedom is being defended, to serve it, and to live or die for it." Casimir came to America as a volunteer, and as such, he was not able to be labeled an official officer rank. He was instrumental in showing George Washington the importance of a strong cavalry, which was Pulaski's claim to fame on the battlefield.

Count Casimir Pulaski. *Courtesy of the New York Public Library.*

Imagine the United States without George Washington. It's interesting to note that without Pulaski's influence, Washington would likely have died in the Battle of Brandywine on September 11,

1777. Washington was surrounded by the British, trapped. Casimir, because of his cavalry experience, was able to brave the battlefield with the aid of thirty men and clear a route for Washington to escape. It was at this point that Washington named Pulaski a brigadier general in the Continental army cavalry, in effect forming the cavalry for the colonists.

Pulaski met his end in the Siege of Savannah, mortally wounded on the battlefield on October 9, 1777. He was attempting to rally the troops, as the Patriots were faltering, and was shot in the side. He is laid to rest beneath a grand monument in the center of Savannah's Monterey Square.

Casimir is only the seventh person in American history made an honorary citizen of the United States.

The Siege of Savannah and the Sorrel Weed House

It was a quick show of things when the British took Savannah in 1778 during the Revolution. In retaliation, on September 16, 1779, colonist troops, with the aid of French and Haitian soldiers, began forming a U-shaped military formation in the woods outside the city.

The commanding French admiral, Comte d'Estaing, was a member of the French navy. He set about assembling his men slowly, planning for attack and the reclamation of Savannah.

Beginning on October 3, ships began bombing the occupied city of Savannah, until October 8, when d'Estaing instigated a full-on attack. It was one of the bloodiest battles of the Revolution. While the battle lasted only fifty-five minutes, it claimed the lives of 244 soldiers, including the much-celebrated Count Pulaski.

Charles Henry Comte d'Estaing. *Courtesy of the New York Public Library.*

Since the battle, numerous archaeological digs have been conducted in the area of Madison Square and beneath the now-famous Sorrel Weed House, where perhaps the most surprising discovery was made. On the land where the Sorrel Weed House now sits was a horse stable and British fortification, protecting the southern end of occupied Savannah. In that spot, a battle trench was found and excavated during a restoration project on the grand Savannah home. Within the trench was found dozens of remains of buried soldiers, cut down in the Siege of Savannah. In the fall of 2017, Revolutionary War bullets were found beneath the home's wine cellar, proving that to live in Savannah's Historic District is to quite literally build your home on history.

Nathanael Greene

The man whom many claim saved the American Revolution was born in Rhode Island in 1742. Nathanael Greene was an impressive soldier with a knack for leadership. He formed the militia in Rhode Island in 1744, was appointed general of the Continental army in 1776 and then was made a major general in 1776 by George Washington.

At the time, there had been no general successful at commanding the southern battalions, including General Robert Howe, who'd lost Savannah to the British, and General Benjamin Lincoln, who lost Charleston—leaving two integral port cities in the hands of England.

George Washington had chosen Nathanael Greene for the task of driving the British away. Greene was at West Point at the time the decision was made and received a message from Washington simply saying, "It is my wish to appoint you."

Leaving his wife, Catharine, and his children behind in Rhode Island, Greene took command at Hillsborough, North Carolina, on December 3, 1780. He is credited with introducing his own unique style of guerrilla warfare to the Revolution, coordinating quick militia groups and leaving British troops surprised and confused. The unexpected and unfamiliar techniques left the British weakened, leading to the Patriots' ability to win the Revolution.

In May 1781, Greene sent troops to Augusta, taking back the Georgian city in less than a month. Then, in 1782, Savannah was taken back as well.

Once the Revolution was won, the government showed its appreciation for Greene's contribution to America's victory by awarding him Mulberry Grove Plantation, just outside Savannah. In 1782, Nathanael moved there with Catharine and their six children. Tragically, he died of heat stroke just a year later while on the plantation.

The Nathanael Greene Memorial in Johnson Square. *Courtesy of the Jeff Bush Photography Collection.*

Nathanael Greene is immortalized in Savannah's Johnson Square with an imposing monument flanked on east and west by two fountains, impossible to miss.

THE WASHINGTON GUNS

In 1791, President George Washington made a very special trip to Savannah. He stayed at the corner of what today is Oglethorpe Avenue and Drayton Streets at the home of Lachlan McIntosh.

It was a happy visit, organized to establish the Order of Cincinnati in Savannah. The order was an exclusive club established in New York in 1783, solely intended for those who served as generals or officers during the American Revolution. The motto of the order was *Omnia reliquit servare rempublicam* ("He relinquished everything to save the Republic").

Washington's arrival to Savannah was celebrated with parades and parties across the city. The trip was a success, and in his gratitude to Savannah's warm welcome and kindness, he sent back two bronze cannons, with the inscription, "Surrendered by the capitulation of York Towne, October 19, 1781." The guns were used in the Battle of Yorktown during the Revolutionary War, captured by Lord Cornwall. According to *The Papers of George Washington*, he also included a letter to the officials of Savannah:

> *Gentlemen, your affectionate congratulations on my arrival in the city,*
> *and the very favorable sentiments you express toward me, are received with*

The Washington Guns.
Courtesy of the Jeff Bush
Photography Collection.

George Washington. *Courtesy of the New York Public Library.*

gratitude and thanked with sincerity. Estimating favors by the cordiality with which they are bestowed, I confess, with real pleasure, my obligation to the Corporation of Savannah, and I can never cease to entertain a grateful sense of their goodness. While the virtuous conduct of your citizens, whose patriotism braved all the hardships of the late war, engaged my esteem, the distresses peculiar to the State of Georgia, after the peace, excited my deepest regret. It was with singular satisfaction I perceived that the efficacy of the general government could interpose effectual relief and restore tranquility to so deserving a member of the Union—Your sentiments on the event are worthy of citizens, who placing a due value on the blessings of peace, desire to maintain it on the immutable principles of justice and good faith. May the harmony of your city be consequent on your administration, and may you individually be happy.

The cannons are an understated, sometimes overlooked treasure of the city of Savannah, protected over the centuries and even buried underground during the Civil War. Visitors to Savannah can see them today, just outside Savannah's capitol building.

MULBERRY GROVE PLANTATION

Hidden in the deep marshy woods twenty-five minutes north of Savannah lie scattered bricks, sunken deep in the mud—almost forgotten, inaccessible. It's a place taken back by nature, a place that once stood proud and huge and bustling with melancholy hands and bales of cotton, a fulcrum piece in the greater story of slavery and plantation life in the South.

It was an innocuous plantation, granted to Nathanael Greene after his services to Washington during the Revolution. Shortly thereafter, the war hero was brought down by an unfortunate run-in with heat stroke. His widow, Catharine, remained there. When the young inventor Eli Whitney came to stay for a season and tutor the Greene children, the difficulty of separating cotton came across his attention. It was no time before he was testing out the early designs of his famous cotton gin.

The cotton gin was patented in 1794, and the machine would be a boon for cotton production and a direct instigator for increased demand for slaves, increased production and, eventually, the heart of a slave-dependent economy that would buckle under the might of the Union.

Eli Whitney's cotton gin, 1793. *Courtesy of the New York Public Library.*

If you drive down the road these days toward the old Mulberry Grove Plantation, you won't see any sign of the historic place except for an unassuming historical marker. The plantation failed, having fallen on hard times, and Catharine Greene sold it. The house was eventually abandoned and fell to ruin.

Slavery in Savannah

The old city as it stands today wouldn't have been possible if it hadn't been for the slave labor that constructed it. Many of the structures that attract visitors from far and wide wouldn't stand now if it weren't for the proud people who endured the worst of human nature and continued on in grace and dignity until the long-awaited days of freedom. They were the cost that came with the boom of the cotton gin. It was their knowledge that cultivated the soil here, and they toiled toward a promise deeper in the heart than human hand could reach. Theirs is a story of captives in an unknown land. A story of grit and survival and hard-fought freedom. Theirs is a legacy that can never be forgotten.

The Long Journey Over

The majority of slaves brought to Savannah's shores were transported from slave markets in the Caribbean, while the remaining came directly from West Africa. The voyage from West Africa to Savannah's shores would have lasted between four and six excruciating months. Slaves were packed closely together beneath the ship's hull, where personal space was all but nonexistent. The prisoners—men, women and children—were often shackled together for the duration of the journey, creating inevitably unsanitary environments. The spread of infectious disease was an unavoidable obstacle, as well as a particular concern once the surviving captives reached their port of destination.

The threat of disease spreading into Savannah was so great that Tybee Island came to play an integral part in the slaves' arrival to Georgia. Lazaretto, an Italian name for "pest house," was a nine-story building constructed on Tybee's western shores where incoming slaves could be quarantined until examined by a physician. Sick and dying prisoners remained there at the house, and those who never recovered from their heartbreaking voyage were buried unceremoniously on the island.

With Oglethorpe's departure in the 1750s, the slave trade grew rapidly in Savannah. The trend continued steadily until new initiatives outlawed slave trade in 1798. The southern economy was so rooted in slave labor, however, that Congressional regulations were not enough to halt the practice. The slave trade continued illegally, and without much pushback, well into the 1800s. The last recorded slave ship to Georgia's shores, just off the nearby Jekyll Island, was the *Wanderer* in 1858, with more than four hundred souls on board.

Once slaves were transported from Lazaretto, they arrived in the city of Savannah, where they were grouped in pens in Johnson Square. At this time, they would have been washed and tended to in an effort to make them look healthy and fit. They would have been branded with hot irons to mark them as slaves, after which they were ready for inspection by interested buyers.

The auctioneer usually decided the opening price for a slave auction, and the sales would have been advertised days in advance to ensure healthy turnouts from the surrounding region. Particularly wealthy landowners could avoid auction dealings by paying slightly higher prices to have first choice of the available slaves the morning before the auction took place.

It was a painful, humiliating time for the slaves involved. They could only hope and pray that the new lives that lay out in front of them would be kinder than popular experience promised.

FROM TOWN TO PLANTATION

The lives of slaves who worked within the city of Savannah versus the ones who lived on plantations just outside of town would have been vastly different.

Downtown living in Savannah during the time of slavery was a crowded and somewhat chaotic situation. Manor houses would have boasted impressive courtyards, most of them bursting with the squawks of chickens, the bleating of goats and the pent-up odor of dairy cows. The street levels were often littered and smelly.

One major difference between urban slaves and plantation slaves was that urban slaves intermingled with free black citizens. It wasn't uncommon for a free black Savannian to be married to a black urban slave. Households mixed with free blacks and enslaved blacks were not unheard of.

Urban slaves had curfews to abide by and lived primarily in carriage houses or street-level apartments. Any time slaves left their homes, they had to carry with them a ticket that described where they were going, what work they were to do that day and what time they were to be home. The slaves were very heavily monitored, to the extent that if their owners left town, they often boarded their slaves in jails to make sure they were still in residence when they came back. Jails were also used for private punishments rather than public displays, which were widely looked down upon.

Secret schools were common in the city of Savannah. Children of slaves would spend as much time as they could in these secret institutions, knowing that literacy would play a key role in obtaining their future freedom and the lives they could build for themselves beyond.

About 10 to 20 percent of Savannah slaves at any given time would have been urban slaves. As seen in Lacey Elizabeth Brooks's "Municipal Slavery," the City of Savannah itself owned slaves, putting them to work on infrastructure and the maintenance of municipal buildings.

Living conditions for urban slaves who lived in slave community housing rather than their owners' homes often comprised single-room huts equipped with a chimney for cooking and community gathering. Conversely, slaves who lived within the homes of their masters were subjected to more solitary and isolated lives, separate from the more communal conditions of other urban or plantation slaves.

The lives of slaves on plantations were particularly different. Depending on how isolated a plantation was, it would have been run like a small village, and the slaves who lived there would have had very distinct roles that kept the plantations running like well-oiled machines. Slaves would have been greeted to a call to work, whether by a horn blowing or a bell being rung. Men would make their ways to the field, overseen by a field driver armed with a whip.

Women worked in the fields often, picking cotton or other goods, while others were consigned to the house, where they oversaw the cooking, cleaning and management of children. Unfortunately, many female house slaves were the victims of physical abuses, both in urban and plantation settings.

Plantation slaves worked as blacksmiths, carpenters and mechanics, their labor becoming integral to the running of the plantation. The more skilled a slave became at a particular craft, the more valuable he became.

Sundays were traditionally days off for slaves, at which time they could attend to their own personal needs and the upkeep of their own dwellings. In the words of the famous Frederick Douglass in his autobiography:

> *There were no beds given to the slaves, unless one coarse blanket be considered such, and none but the men and women had these. They find less difficulty from the want of beds, than from the want of time to sleep; for when their days work in the field is done, the most of them having their washing, mending, and cooking to do, and having few or none of the ordinary facilities for doing wither of these, very many of their sleeping hours are consumed in preparing for the field the coming day; and when this is done, old and young, male and female, married and single, drop down side by side, on one common bed—the cold, damp floor—each covering himself or herself with their miserable blankets; and here they sleep til they are summoned to the field by the driver's horn.*

MOTHER MATHILDA BEASLEY

In the early hours of the day, it was common to see groups of small black children walking the streets of Savannah, seemingly on the way to work. But their true destination was often a secret school, most likely in a free person's private home. The children would change their routes to school daily, hiding their books carefully. Black education was banned in urban Savannah, but that didn't stop people like Julien Fromatin, James Porter, Mary Woodhouse, Jane Deveaux or James Sims, all of whom were brave teachers at the time, committed to instructing enslaved children under the cover of secrecy.

Punishment for those caught teaching black children was $500 for white teachers, and a $100 fine and thirty lashes for black teachers. Regardless, the schools were more or less run as "open secrets." Despite the laws against educating young black children, many slave owners didn't mind literacy among their slaves, particularly urban slaves, as it made them more capable and efficient at their work within the city.

One free African American woman was at the forefront of educating young slaves and free black children, Mother Mathilda Beasley. She ran her secret school for a decade, from 1850 to 1860, from her home in downtown Savannah. Mathilda was orphaned at a young age by her enslaved mother in New Orleans, at which time she made her way to Savannah and worked as a seamstress and waitress in the 1850s within the free black community. It was during this time that she opened her secret school. Mathilda was baptized at the Cathedral of St. John the Baptist in 1869, after which she married her Catholic fiancé, Abraham Beasley.

The owner of a successful Savannah restaurant, Abraham was a very wealthy African American man who, some speculate, had been involved in the slave trade at one time. He died in 1877, leaving his full estate to Mathilda. As the couple did not have any children, she donated the wealth in full to the Catholic Church, perhaps in penitence for the slave trade that contributed to the wealth. Shortly after, Mathilda moved to England and joined an order of nuns. She came back to Savannah and established the St. Francis Home for Colored Orphans in 1887. She was also the founder of the very first community of African American nuns in 1889. Mathilda continued to work as a seamstress, her earnings going to support Savannah's poor until she passed away in 1903 at the age of seventy-one.

WEEPING TIME

It was the largest sale of human beings in the history of the United States. In a city of breathtaking beauty, struggling ideals and grand hopes for the future, there was plenty of cruelty and heartbreak to be found.

It was bitterly cold and rainy on March 2 and 3, 1859, when the largest sale of slaves in Georgia history took place. Signer of the U.S. Constitution Pierce Butler of Darian, Georgia, sold 436 men, women and children. He needed to pay back his creditors and clear his debts, so he sold slaves at an average cost of $700 per person, making a little more than $300,000, which translates to more than $6 million today. The dark days came to be known as the "Weeping Time."

Joseph Bryan was a notorious slave dealer in Savannah, known for coordinating the sale of slaves. He maintained slave pens in Johnson Square and established slave brokerage offices nearby, where he conducted sales. Bryan oversaw Weeping Time, which had to be located at the race grounds outside town to accommodate the vast number of souls for sale. In the days leading up to the sale, interested purchasers could visit the grounds where the slaves were held to inspect the slaves for health and desirable physical attributes.

As found in *Slavery and Freedom in Savannah*, an ad run by Bryan in the Savannah papers the *Republican* and the *Savannah Morning News* on February 8, 1859, read:

> For Sale. Long Cotton and Rice Negroes. A gang of 460 negroes, accustomed to the culture of rice and provisions; among whom are a number of good mechanics, and house servants. Will be sold on the 2^d and 3^d of March next, at Savannah, by Joseph Bryan. Terms of Sale—One third cash; remainder by bond, bearing interest from day of sale. Payable in two equal annual installments, to be secured by mortgage on the negroes, and approved personal security, or for approved city acceptance on Savannah or Charleston. Purchasers paying for papers. The negroes will be sold in families, and can be seen on the premises of Joseph Bryan, in Savannah. Three days prior to the day of sale, when catalogues will be furnished.

According to PBS's "The Weeping Time: Africans in America," entire lives, dreams of freedom found together, dreams of a future, loves meant to last a lifetime, were ripped apart in the space of two days, as noted in Philadelphia socialite Sidney George Fisher's diary:

> It is a dreadful affair, however, selling these hereditary negroes…families will not be separated, that is to say, husbands and wives, parents and young children. But brothers and sisters of mature age, parents and children of mature age, all other relations and the ties of home and long association will be violently severed. It will be a hard thing for Butler to witness and it is a monstrous thing to do. Yet is it done every day in the South. It is one among the many frightful consequences of slavery and contradicts our civilization, our Christianity, or Republicanism. Can such a system endure? Is it consistent with humanity, with moral progress? There are difficult questions and still more difficult is it to say, what can be done? The negroes of the South must be slaves, or the South will become Africanized, Slavery is better for them and for us than such a result.

Well-known journalist Mortimer Thompson wrote of the sale, "On the faces of all was an expression of heavy grief; some appeared to be resigned to the hard stroke of Fortune that had torn them from their homes, and were sadly trying to make the best of it; some sat brooding

Young chimney sweeps, 1870. *Courtesy of the New York Public Library.*

moodily over their sorrows, their chins resting on their hands, their eyes staring vacantly, and their bodies rocking to and fro, with a restless motion that was never stilled."

It's one of the darkest recorded events in Savannah's history.

THE FIRST AFRICAN BAPTIST CHURCH

Not only is the First African Baptist Church a key landmark of Savannah's African American culture, but it was also a treasured stopping point along the Underground Railroad. The founder of the congregation was a freed slave, George Liele, an ordained minister who traveled along the Savannah River, converting slaves to Christianity. The church itself was officially begun in 1788, led by minister Andrew Bryan.

Andrew Cocksmarshall became the reverend following Andrew Bryan. He had a vision in 1832 that he needed to purchase the land where another wooden church presently stood, to build a new church "large and of brick." After much sacrifice, the congregation made up of freed and enslaved blacks was able to raise the more than $1,000 needed to make the purchase, most of the monies coming from enslaved men and women who'd been saving up to purchase their freedom. It was a victorious if not bold effort. They changed the name of the church from First Colored Baptist to First African Baptist, paying off all they owed on November 1, 1832.

In 1855, they started fresh construction on the brick structure that stands today. The slaves' masters gave them permission to build their brick church, but only at night once the day's work was done. They made the brick used for the church, today known as Savannah gray brick, by hand at the banks of the Savannah River. Once the brick was set, women

The First African Baptist Church. *Courtesy of the Jeff Bush Photography Collection.*

would carry the bricks up the bluff and all the way to the construction site, where they would then tend bonfires, so the men could see to work. They completed the building in 1859, four very patient years later.

It was during the construction that they discovered underground tunnels that they used as hiding places along the Underground Railroad.

Today, holes can still be seen in the floor of the church that form diamond-shaped patterns called *kongo cosmogram*, totaling thirty-six holes that symbolized it as a stop along the secret route. Slaves would hide in four-foot spaces beneath the floorboards during worship services, making their way out with guardians who helped them blend into the crowd once services were over. The church was regularly used as a safe haven for escaped slaves, which set it apart among other churches that were afraid to put their congregations at risk.

GROWING PAINS

The Civil War and Savannah

It was the election of 1860 and Abraham Lincoln was vying for the presidential ticket. He ran with a campaign message against slavery, which meant his chance of winning the South was next to none. The South was booming economically, with Savannah's success mostly due to cotton exports (the second-strongest in the world)—and all of it riding on the back of slave labor and Mr. Whitney's cotton gin.

It was a time of lavish Savannah parties and unapologetic excess. A time when the southern people of power didn't fancy the idea of making any changes. They had it good, and they intended to keep it that way.

ALEXANDER H. STEPHENS

Lincoln had not yet been president for a month. It was March 21, 1861, and Alexander H. Stephens (who later became the vice-president of the Confederate States of America from 1861 to 1865) gave one of the most repulsive speeches of his career in Savannah's beautiful Chippewa Square at the Savannah Theater, then called the Athenaeum.

It was 7:30 pm. and Chippewa Square had never seen a crowd as large or as chaotic. Stephens arrived, and the mayor of Savannah at the time, the Honorable C.C. Jones, officially introduced Mr. Stephens to the theater and asked for silence at the doors. The problem was that there were more people

Savannah, Georgia, 1856. *Courtesy of the New York Public Library.*

outside the theater than inside of it, and they were desperate to hear what Stevens had to say. The mayor made the excuse that Stephens's health would not permit him to give the speech outside, most likely for security purposes, at which time Stephens offered to assuage the crowd and brave the outside air. The ladies inside the theater erupted in protest, not wanting to leave the theater themselves. And so, it was finally settled that for the sake of the women, the speech would take place inside the Athenaeum.

Local dignitaries were seated near the stage. As found in *Alexander H. Stephens, in Public and Private*, Stephens began by thanking them for being there:

> *"When perfect quiet is restored I shall proceed," he said. In what came to be called The Cornerstone Speech, Stephens claimed, "our new government is founded upon exactly the opposite idea* [the Declaration of Independence] *its foundations are laid, its cornerstone rests, upon the great truth that the negro is not equal to the white man, that slavery, subordination to the superior race, is his natural and normal condition. This, our new government, is the first, in the history of the world, based upon this great physical, philosophical, and moral truth. This truth has been slow in the process of its development, like all other truths in the various departments of science.... They* [the North] *assume the Negro is equal, and hence conclude that he is entitled to equal privileges and rights*

Savannah's Chippewa Square in 1901. *Courtesy of the New York Public Library.*

with the white man. If their premises were correct, their conclusions would be logical and just, but their premise being wrong, their whole argument fails....With us all of the white race, however high or low, rich or poor, are equal in the eye of the law. Not so with the Negro. Subordination is his place."

The original purpose of the speech was supposed to have been to explain the new constitution of the Confederacy, but the speech went on to solidify Stephens in infamy. Following the speech Stephens rarely met with Jefferson Davis, the president of the Confederacy, perhaps as a result of the speech's extremely divisive nature.

A member of the Democratic Party, Stephens was the fiftieth governor of Georgia, from 1882 until his death in 1883. After the Civil War ended, Stephens unsuccessfully attempted to retract his statements.

WARTIME WOMEN OF SAVANNAH

The vast majority of women in Savannah—and Georgia at large—urged their husbands to leave the Union army after the election of Abraham Lincoln in 1860. Georgian women felt that it was their right as Southerners to have the lifestyle they wanted. The upper class, generally slaveholding, was a particular supporter of the war.

Once the war started, young able-bodied men left town in an exodus to join the fight, and so poorer women were put to work, replacing the men in positions of daily society.

In 1862, the Union army took over Fort Pulaski, cutting off the main river routes to Savannah. Goods and basic household wares, including dresses, clothes and furniture—anything that the ladies of Savannah were used to receiving as imports—were suddenly at a deficit. According to the diary of Mrs. Josephine C. Habersham in 1863, "$58 for summer muslin, $195 for a dress I could have got two years ago for just $9. $60 for a straw bonnet—untrimmed!" The cost of goods in the South indeed skyrocketed, as demand well outweighed supply, which served to make an already unbearable time even more uncomfortable.

The Southern women who had pushed so hard for war suffered terribly, with many of them called on to make sacrifices they hadn't bargained for. Food pantry lines, a society in shambles—it was a tough, inescapable reality.

As the war progressed, tensions rose and supplies grew leaner, and as the Union finally suffocated the South, women who weren't wealthy to begin with became desperate; many resorted to looting and riots to feed their starving families. By the time Sherman and his Union troops arrived, the women of Savannah fairly seethed with hatred. Except, of course, the few Union sympathizers trapped in the Southern city, like Nellie Gordon, the mother of Girl Scouts founder Juliette Gordon Low. She tried her best to keep her sentiments to herself even after her uncle, Union general William Hunter, took Fort Pulaski.

John Underwood revealed in *The Women of the Confederacy* that women often saw the bloody truth of war firsthand, as random homes and establishments were converted into hospitals, filled to the brim with the nearly dead and dying. But despite the South being brought low, women's gumption and tenacity didn't escape the attention of William Sherman himself, who said, "You women are the toughest set I ever knew. The men would have given up long ago, but for you. I believe you would have kept up this war for thirty years."

DR. RICHARD ARNOLD AND THE SURRENDER OF SAVANNAH

In November 1864, General William T. Sherman led his army of between sixty-two thousand and sixty-five thousand soldiers out of a burnt Atlanta. He split the regiments into two large brigades of thirty thousand plus, commanding them to head for Savannah, the last Southern bastion by the sea, and destroy all property in their path.

Upon leaving Atlanta, Sherman went a bit rogue, cutting all ties of communication with the North save for a letter he wrote in which, according to Joseph Ewing's "The New Sherman Letters," he said, "If my name must go to history, I prefer it should not as the enemy to the south, or any system of labor which however objectionable has cleared the forest and cornbreaks and developed a wealth otherwise latent, but against mobs, vigilance committees, and all the other phases of sedition and anarchy which have threatened and still endanger the country which our children must inhabit."

Meanwhile, in a heavily guarded Savannah, led by General William J. Hardee, the city knew that its fate was a head-on clash with William Sherman's ever-approaching army. According to the U.S. War Department, on December 17, 1864, General Sherman sent word to General Hardee that Savannah should be surrendered before his arrival: "Should you entertain the proposition, I am prepared to grant liberal terms to the inhabitants and garrison; but should I be forced to resort to assault, or the slower and sure process of starvation, I shall then feel justified in resorting to the harshest measures. And shall make little effort to restrain my army—burning to avenge the national wrong which they attach to Savannah and other large cities which have been so prominent in dragging our country into Civil War."

Surprisingly to many, General Hardee refused surrender to Sherman, but he didn't stand against the Northern general either. Rather, he quickly prepared his soldiers to abandon Savannah and retreated from Sherman's wrath on the morning of December 21, 1864.

Left to his own devices was the ever-stalwart mayor of Savannah, Dr. Richard Arnold, and his more than twenty-two thousand residents, now defenseless and vulnerable to attack. Dr. Arnold and a group of aldermen, with reportedly no military training at all, dashed into the marsh in Sherman's path, hoping for a meeting before the general reached the city of Savannah. Rather than meeting with Sherman face to face, Arnold found that the first arriving point of contact for the Union was General John Geary, who was well known for aiding the Union victory in Gettysburg. Dr. Arnold officially read out loud to Geary a proclamation of surrender and a request for his protection over the lives and property of Savannah's citizens.

John Geary accepted Dr. Arnold's request. Dr. Richard Arnold then requested the citizens of Savannah to return to business as usual, accommodating the Union soldiers and doing what was necessary to secure Savannah's continued safety. As sixty-five thousand troops rolled into the city, the majority of locals were women peering out of windows, hiding their valuables and mustering their bravest faces and most beguiling Southern hospitality.

GENERAL JOHN W. GEARY

The news of Atlanta had shaken those still in Sherman's path to their core. The Confederacy was on its deathbed, and as far as Southern morale was concerned, the end was near.

General John Geary was born in Mount Pleasant, modern-day Pittsburgh, Pennsylvania, on December 30, 1819. He was an imposing man, a sight to behold for his time, standing at a reported six and a half feet tall and well over two hundred pounds. He was also incredibly smart.

Closing in on Savannah just ahead of General Sherman, Geary knew that he'd arrive to find the people of Savannah terrified. Upon his approach of the city, Geary was met by Savannah's mayor, Dr. Richard Arnold, who was prepared to do whatever necessary to spare Savannah from General Sherman's flames.

Geary served as something of a diplomat between Savannah and the Union army, successfully arranging for the peaceful surrender of the city. Once Sherman arrived and it was decided that Savannah would blessedly not be burned to the ground, Geary was assigned as acting military governor of Savannah during Sherman's time here.

It was his temporary governance that is credited with the great continued preservation of the city of Savannah, despite the residence of thousands of Union troops within its borders, all of them well accustomed to looting and pillaging. Instead, during the Union's rather uninvited tenure, Geary arranged for parades and parties held downtown. He acted kindly toward the locals, who expressed their concerns to him, in many ways a buffer between the frightened people and the still terrifying General Sherman, who held all their fates in his hands.

But it wasn't just civility Geary was after. Savannah was an important port city for the Union to control, effectively cutting off supplies to the Confederacy—a task Geary oversaw until the Union was declared victorious. Years later, Geary became governor of Pennsylvania in 1867.

The Greene-Meldrim House, Edwin Stanton and the Meeting that Changed Everything

On January 12, 1865, a meeting was called to the Charles Greene House on Madison Square. It was 8:00 p.m. In the cold darkness of night, twenty men entered the home—twenty black ministers and pastors, eleven of them freed.

They were greeted by General William Sherman and Edwin Stanton, secretary of war and President Lincoln's counselor. Edwin Stanton asked a series of questions sent down to Savannah straight from President Lincoln. One question in particular changed everything: "State on what manner you think you can take care of yourself, and how can you best assist the government in maintaining your freedom?"

According to Steven Miller's "Newspaper Account of a Meeting Between Black Religious Leaders and Union Military Authorities," sixty-seven-year-old Garrison Frazier, a free man who purchased his and his wife's freedom for $1,000, responded first: "The way we can best take care of ourselves is to have land, and turn it and till it by our own labor…that is, by the labor of the women, and children, and old men…and we can soon maintain ourselves and have something to spare.…We want to be placed on land until we are able to buy it and make it our own."

More questions followed. "State what is the feeling of colored people in regard to General Sherman; and how far do they regard his sentiments and actions as friendly to their rights and interests, or otherwise?" They answered:

> *We looked upon General Sherman prior to his arrival as a man in the Providence of God specially set apart to accomplish this work, and we unanimously feel inexpressible gratitude to him, looking upon him as a man that should be honored for the faithful performance of his duty. Some of us called upon him immediately upon his arrival, and it is probable he would not meet the Secretary with more courtesy than he met us. His conduct*

and deportment toward us characterized him as a friend and a gentleman. We have confidence in General Sherman and think that what concerns us could not be under better hands. This is our opinion now from the short acquaintance and interest we have had.

Here was the answer to an immediate question—what to do with the refugees who had walked with Sherman south to Savannah. Written by Sherman and revised by Stanton, four days later on the footsteps of Savannah's First African Baptist Church Special Field Order 15 was read aloud, in which President Lincoln granted enslaved families forty acres each:

By the laws of war, and orders of the President of the United States, the negro is free, and must be dealt with as such, he cannot be subjected to conscription, or forced military service, save by the written orders of the highest military authority of the department, under such regulations as the President or congress may prescribe. Domestic servants, blacksmiths, carpenters, and other mechanics will be free to select their own work and residence, but the young and able-bodied negroes must be encouraged to

The Green-Meldrim House. *Courtesy of the Jeff Bush Photography Collection.*

enlist as soldiers in the service of The United States, to contribute their share toward maintaining their own freedom and securing their rights as citizens of The United States.

At the time, there were forty thousand slaves who immediately benefited, made up of Savannah's city and regional enslaved, and about seventeen thousand refugees who had marched with Sherman to the sea. The initial amount of acreage granted was forty thousand acres that ran thirty miles inland from the coast of Charleston to the St. Johns River in Florida.

It was the turning of a tide, a both symbolic and literal occurrence that reshaped the future of not only the South but also an entire nation. The trickle-down effect of the order was immediate. Once the freed slaves left their plantations, the landowners had neither the skill or manpower to maintain agricultural production. It was the final nail in the coffin of the Confederacy.

The Civil War functionally ended with the surrender at Appomattox on April 9, 1865. President Lincoln died six days later.

PIN POINT: THE PRIDE OF THE FREE

The site began as Beulieu Plantation, the home of William Stephens, second governing leader of Savannah after whose death slavery entered the colony. Perhaps fittingly, it was also where one thousand newly freed slaves, led by Ulysses L. Houston, gathered and plotted out their new lives after Special Field Order 15. Houston was forty-one years old at the time, a slave up until the Union occupation, and was pastor of Savannah's Third African Baptist Church. He became the first governor of the newly freed black community settled at Pin Point, possibly named for the trees that grow there called chinquapin.

The residents of Pin Point remained direct descendants of Savannah's slaves, fiercely upholding the heritage of the Geechee—the captive people who built the foundation of the South that stands today. They had been the ones who knew how to grow the rice, indigo and cotton and work the land. Their hands were the ones that made the earth thrive. And their relationship with the land has continued on over the centuries.

Gullah-Geechee culture today remains centered at Pin Point, and many of the beautiful influences of the African culture there are enjoyed across the

South and beyond in the forms of southern food, art, music and Lowcountry island aesthetic. Many of the traditions are rooted in the long history of West Africa and Western Sudan, the heritages of most of the southerly American slaves. Ring Shouts, for example, no longer practiced today, were religious ceremonies where slaves converted to Christianity danced together in circles, shouting and dancing, happily welcoming possession by the Holy Spirit. The dance mirrored traditional African ceremonies and was a beautiful example of the unique flavors of the Geechee culture.

Southern food enjoyed by the platter-full today—like fried foods, hush puppies, spicy seafoods and gumbos—were all derived from menus created from slave rations comprising things like rice and peas, sweet potatoes, mackerel, molasses, pork, bacon, meal and grits. The foods that developed were delectable amalgamations of cultures from opposite sides of the ocean.

Guests to Pin Point today hear the musicality of great-grandfathers passing along an almost lost Gullah language. So many cultures from Africa were brought over to America at once that there was a clash of many African languages and dialects, not to mention the business of learning English, the language of their masters. A language comprising English slang, as well as common derivatives of African terms, developed to make communication within the African American culture easier. The Gullah language developed, with words like *ooman*, meaning "woman"; *day clean*, meaning "dawn"; *krack teet*, meaning to talk, describing the sound teeth make when someone is speaking; *wegitubble*, meaning "vegetable"; and *gwine*, meaning "going." It's an intuitive and musical language, often described as "Sea Island Creole."

The Gullah-Geechees' continued artistry of net-making, sweet grass basket weaving, culinary secrets and storytelling are irreplaceable treasures of Savannah's emerald shores. The Gullah coast spans from Amelia Island all the way north to Charleston.

FROGTOWN

After the Civil War, many freed slaves settled in an area of Savannah called Frogtown, named for the local wildlife. Today, it's marked by MLK Boulevard, but at that time, it would have been along West Broad Street.

Now free, the former slaves' families grew, and they built their own businesses, bought and sold their own goods and lived and died by their own

Unidentified African American woman and a young man, probably her son, at their home in 1890. *Courtesy of the New York Public Library.*

rules. They managed their own successes and their own failures. Frogtown became a booming success—Savannah's version of New York City's Harlem.

Restaurants, theaters, nightclubs and homes all sprang up together. They illuminated the western side of Savannah for the following decades. It was a tightknit community, where the bonds of family extended to the next-door neighbors and one man's problem would be met with the solutions of many.

The challenges came when the old Union Train Station was torn down in 1963. The station was replaced with an overpass, essentially dividing Frogtown from the rest of downtown Savannah. Today, visitors might catch a glimpse of an old sign or reference to Frogtown, but almost nothing of the old district's distinction is left.

Savannah Welcomes the Twentieth Century

The war had brought Savannah to its knees, and the old ways of Georgia were no more. The Union army had decimated the Southern economy, setting the region back decades. But over time, the cities were rebuilt, and Savannah, blessedly spared from Sherman's fires, found its old sparkle. Cotton production picked back up, and wealth and opportunity returned to the people.

Even through the First World War, Savannah stood strong and weathered the loss of more young men. But more hard times were on the horizon, seemingly intent against the Hostess City and its heart of fire.

The Savannah Cotton Exchange: The (Haughty) Deep Breath Before the Plunge

In its antebellum heyday, Savannah was once known as the Wall Street of the South—all because of white gold, the South's precious cotton. It was the post–Civil War boon. In 1872 alone, $40 million of revenue was brought into the city, as the leading exporter of cotton in the United States, second-leading exporter in the world. It felt only appropriate to build a center for this cotton.

The original architect of the Savannah Cotton Exchange, William Preston, won the bid for the design, and construction on the project was

The Savannah Cotton Exchange. *Courtesy of the Jeff Bush Photography Collection.*

completed in 1886. The Cotton Exchange was, and is, central to Factor's Walk, in which today's visitors will notice a series of iron bridges hovering over a maze of alleyways. Above those cobblestone walkways was once a bustling frenzy of loading cotton onto ships for export, as managers and overseers stood on the bridges overhead, ledgers open, counting the bales and loaded wagons one by one.

The Cotton Exchange still stands as a symbol of Savannah's resilience and industry. Interestingly, despite its aged appearance, the lion statue that perches in front of the Cotton Exchange today is not the original lion installed in 1890. The current lion is a replica designed in 2009 after a car accident shattered the original.

THE HOTEL DESOTO

The opulent Hotel DeSoto once stood as the jewel of Liberty Street. The grand building played host to parties and galas, famous visitors to Savannah, countless weddings and nights of adventure, entertainment and intrigue.

Savannah's goal for the hotel was a luxury stop on the route for those bound to Florida. At a cost of $410,000, the hotel opened on New Year's Day 1890 at almost twice the original estimated cost. Fitted with tennis courts, mini golf, sunrooms, barbershops and ballrooms, the DeSoto was the place to be seen in Savannah. Its architecture was influenced by opulent hotels to the North, with an eye toward splendor.

The Hotel DeSoto, Savannah, Georgia. *Courtesy of the New York Public Library.*

Over the years, guests included five presidents, Hollywood celebrities and sports stars including Babe Ruth. Air conditioning was added to the hotel, as well as a swimming pool, in 1923. Savannah's first radio station premiered on the top floor of the hotel in 1926.

And then World War II happened. Families were pulled to the suburbs, and downtown Savannah fell to neglect—and the splendorous hotel with it. The DeSoto was torn down in 1966, with officials citing that restorations to the historic building would be too expensive. Developers had an eye toward modern architecture in a bid to bring fresh attention to the southern city, and so the hotel was demolished and rebuilt, completely unrecognizable, in 1968.

JULIET GORDON LOW: BRINGING GIRLS INTO THE NEXT CENTURY

Hers is a name celebrated by young girls and women the nation over. Juliet Gordon Low was the daughter of William and Nellie Gordon, destined to marry the wealthy Andrew Low and travel abroad for a life of adventure and gumption. Juliet was the founder of the Girl Scouts, holding the first ever meeting in the carriage house of the Andrew Low House.

Not many know the unique and adventurous history of the woman who would champion women's rights before it was popular to do so. She was born in the house on the corner of today's Bull Street and Oglethorpe Avenue in Savannah, Georgia, on October 31, 1860. Juliet's uncle held her in his arms and said, "What a pretty little daisy." The nickname stuck for the rest of her life. Juliet lived a comfortable life with her family up until the Civil War, when she and her siblings were sent north to ride out the conflict.

Juliet grew a spine of steel. At seventeen, she came down with an ear infection. Silver nitrate was used to try and heal her ear, which resulted in hearing loss. When she was twenty-six, she married William Low, the son of Andrew Low, the wealthy shipping merchant. While Juliet came from railroad money, her husband's wealthy was in cotton.

It was just following their wedding ceremony when a piece of rice was thrown and lodged in Juliet's ear. She didn't wish to have it removed and ruin her honeymoon. When it came time to finally dislodge the piece of rice, the tool that the doctor used caused damage to her ear, resulting in hearing loss in that ear too. Despite being deaf, Juliet had a talent for reading lips, and many who came in contact with her didn't realize that she couldn't hear them.

William was known as a social butterfly, and the young couple moved to England, far from Juliet's parents, who weren't fully supportive of the match. The two lived in Warwickshire, enjoying life, but Juliet was determined to get her hearing back and ended up spending time traveling to meet doctors away from her husband. William took a mistress named Anna Bateman. Juliet knew of Anna, even when William asked for a divorce. By 1905, right before the divorce was finalized, William passed away of a seizure after nineteen years of marriage. Sadly for Juliet, William left his estate to Anna Bateman, leaving Juliet with nothing.

Juliet contested the will, spending her time traveling for the next few years. It was during a trip to Scotland that she met Sir Robert Baden Powell, the founder of the Boy Scouts. After learning that Robert had six thousand secret girls enrolled in his Scouts, Juliet was inspired to start a club for girls. She began the Girl Guides with Robert's sister soon after.

Soon after, an agreement was settled between Juliet and her in-laws, in which she received $500,000 and their home back in Savannah, Georgia.

The Andrew Low House. *Courtesy of the Jeff Bush Photography Collection.*

Juliet moved back to Savannah in 1912 and hosted the first troop meeting with eighteen girls in the carriage house behind her home. It was 1913 when she changed the name of her club from Girl Guides to Girl Scouts.

Juliet passed away in the master bedroom of the Andrew Low House in 1927.

SAVANNAH AND THE GREAT DEPRESSION: A TRIPLE THREAT

By the 1920s, most of the country had rebounded from World War I, and the economy was once again thriving. But not in Savannah and its surrounding areas.

Economic troubles abounded, including a three-year drought beginning in 1925, on the heels of which a boll weevil infestation took out the cotton industry, an absolutely staggering loss to the region. The invention of products like Rayon had already reduced the overall price of cotton. It was clear that changes had to be made. Savannah needed a new industry and fast. Unfortunately, the stock market crashed on October 29, 1929, Black Tuesday, and Savannah was nearly done for.

Despite the worst drought to ever hit southern Georgia in 1930–31, downtown Savannah had it slightly easier than surrounding areas, due to its ports and exports. But the city was hanging on by a thread. And then the world went to war a second time, and Savannah was saved.

WORLD WAR II SAVANNAH

The South had been brought to its knees. Savannah was among the nation's most struggling economies, a problem that had garnered national attention. But once the United States entered into World War II following the attack on Pearl Harbor in 1941, things changed for Savannah fast.

With the need for supplies, weapons and, most of all, ships, Savannah's port was needed to fill a tall order. The job was to produce Liberty ships, important cargo vessels for the U.S. military. The original order was for thirty-six ships, but fifteen thousand workers at Savannah's Southeastern Shipyard ultimately produced eighty-eight Liberty Ships for the United States war effort.

Savannah's Southeastern Shipyard covered more than one hundred acres, boasted its own fire department and became famous for producing the Liberty ships that Roosevelt called his "Ugly Ducklings." Men and women migrated from all across the country to aid in the shipbuilding, which in turn stimulated Savannah's housing industry, which trickled into the Savannah economy at large.

Savannah was once again back on its feet. Today, people who travel down Savannah's Islands Expressway toward Tybee will notice rows of small houses on the south side of the road, just outside town. These are all that's left of the vibrant shipyard. A quiet reminder of the resilience of a port town and brave days gone by.

W.W. Law

W.W. Law was known to many as "Mr. Civil Rights." His name was Westley Wallace Law. He was born poor in Savannah in 1923. After his father died when Law was ten, he entered the workforce, helping his mother support his two younger sisters. His mother and grandmother were his greatest influences, making sure that he was exposed to education and issues of social justice. With a passion to defeat segregation, W.W. became a member of the NAACP Youth Council in high school. From that time forward, he became a voice for justice, equality and peaceful protest. Upon return from serving his country in World War II, Law received a degree in biology from Savannah State University, then known as Georgia State College.

Rather than entering a career related to the sciences, Law became a United States Postal Service mail carrier, a career he kept for more than forty years. From 1950 until 1976, W.W. was the president of the Savannah NAACP, earning the respect of local officials, city councilmen, Dr. Martin Luther King Jr. and even President John F. Kennedy.

Law was most known for peaceful, nonviolent protests. His goal was to affect the core of Savannah business owners. On March 16, 1960, a young woman, Carolyn Quilloin, was arrested for asking for service at a lunch counter at Levy's Department Store. As a response, W.W. Law led sit-ins over an eighteen-month boycott of Broughton Street businesses, forcing local business owners and leaders to recognize the importance of desegregation and honoring the black community as integral members of society.

At that time, Mayor Malcolm Maclean worked with W.W. Law to integrate public buildings, lunch volunteers and libraries and tear down segregation signs that once rent a tear in the fabric of Savannah society. However, some people were opposed to Law's efforts. He was fired from his career as a postal worker in 1961. With the endorsement of President John F. Kennedy, among others rising to his defense, Law was given back his job.

W.W. Law received many honorary doctorates and went on to establish African American heritage museums in Savannah, including the Beech Institute of African American Culture, the Ralph Mark Gilbert Civil Rights Museum, King-Tysdell Cottage Museum and the Negro Heritage Trail Tour.

This was an ordinary man from a poor neighborhood who was raised on a solid foundation of love and courage. He embodied the American right to fight for freedom and equality to argue for the voices of the oppressed without the use of violence. He went on to be one of the most respected men of the civil rights era.

W.W. Law died on July 29, 2002. His gravestone reads, "I was the result of a composite contribution. I tried not to have a big ending, but rather, to live my life doing the best that I could each day, because a good name is rather to be chosen than great riches. A man is poor, not because he doesn't have money, but because he doesn't have enough vision in his head and heart."

Preservation and Architecture

T he world wars were over. Prosperity and peace were at last the
order of the day. But with new sentiments and the reinvention of
what made up a successful modern family, people were moving
away from cities at large in favor of the suburbs and freedom of the quiet
countryside.

And so Savannah's old resplendent houses fell slowly into disarray.
There was little sign of the glamour of the past, the extravagant parties,
the rushes of adventure and the drums of war. It was almost as though the
city had grown tired, as if the worldwide chaos had left it haggard, unable
to remember the vision it had been once. It was a shell of its old splendor,
a whisper of a time long past when people thought about things like honor
for the sake of it. Front porches lined with flowers, tea pots at the ready,
excitement and industry—it was gone, or at least almost.

Too much had happened. And Savannah fell asleep. Maybe it needed the
break—to grow quiet for a while, fold back into itself and slow down. But it
wasn't long before the live oaks caught eyes again, invited fresh adventurers,
and old friends to come and see, to explore and uncover what had been and
what grew—all the lessons that had been learned.

Savannah cast its spell again. And fresh-hearted people came.

The Great Preservation

It all began with the efforts of one passionate woman from Bay Street: Anna Colquitt Hunter. As a young lady, she had worked as a field director for the Red Cross, caring for soldiers coming home from combat. Following the death of her husband, the mother of three built a career as a successful writer for the *Savannah Morning News*, covering Savannah's society groups. Her interest in preservation began from noticing fallen balconies and neglected structures around her home in downtown Savannah.

Miss Hunter also noticed the city's solution of tearing down old structures and replacing them with parking lots to encourage the newly modernized suburbanites back into town. Having witnessed the tearing down of Savannah's Old City Market in 1953, Anna grew increasingly more alarmed and concerned for her beautiful city. What spurred her into action was the following year, when the owners of the now acclaimed Kehoe House wanted to purchase the adjacent historic Davenport House and replace it with a parking lot for their funeral home.

Because of her experience covering the society pages, Anna knew who the powerful women of Savannah were. She assembled a dream team of saviors: Katherine Judkins Clark, Elinor Adler Dillard, Lucy Barrow McIntire, Dorothy Ripley Roebling, Nola McEvoy Roos and Jane Adair Wright. Together, with her fellow concerned ladies of Savannah, Anna raised awareness to the travesties occurring in downtown and launched the Historic Savannah Foundation officially in 1955. The foundation immediately raised the money needed to purchase the Davenport House, saving it forever from threat of demolition.

The Historic Savannah Foundation has continued on its noble mission ever since, restoring and repurposing myriad Savannah properties, bringing back the splendor of Savannah's Historic District.

Haint Blue and Such

On any given day, a walk in Savannah's Historic District is an opportunity to take in hidden symbolism from the past. Perhaps one of the most recognizable, not to mention popular, details is the incorporation of Haint Blue. The word *haint* is old slang meaning ghost. It was commonly used in the region for centuries, derived from the Gullah-Geechee language of the colonial era.

The belief in ghosts in Savannah runs strong—very strong—so it's not a strange occurrence to encounter perfectly logical people going out of their way to banish, and/or keep, the lingering dead from their homes. The old belief is that ghosts can't cross over water, so beginning with the Gullah, the tradition of painting the threshold of their homes in a pale blue paint, almost like a chalk paint, was born. The color was meant to confuse and deter ghosts.

Over time, the colonists adopted the practice, and Haint Blue started to pop up everywhere, from front porches to shutters and even entire rooms. Interior rooms, such as birthing rooms or children's rooms, were being coated in the pale blue color. Today, Haint Blue is still a popular style choice. Surprisingly, the color has been shone to cut down on gnats on front porches, adding to the already charming appeal.

PINEAPPLES

Throughout Savannah's architecture, you'll notice the design of beautiful stone pineapples. The tradition of the pineapple began in the colonial days, when it was a rare fruit, so to present someone with a pineapple was a rare and treasured treat and a particularly honorable gift of welcome.

In the Caribbean, it originally signified that you'd made it home safely from a seafaring adventure. Sailors would set the fruit on their front porch or windowsill as an invitation to their neighbors to come say hello.

Over the centuries, the tradition evolved. When house guests arrived for any extended length of stay, a pineapple would be presented and put on display in the center of the dining table and left there for days. Whenever the host wanted to signify that it was time for their guests to leave, they would simply order the pineapple sliced up and present it to eat with breakfast.

The tradition is still practiced—good-naturedly, of course—in many Savannah homes today.

DOLPHIN FISH

Dolphin fish are a traditional symbol of good luck in the Lowcountry, and so dolphin fish sculptures are commonly set on the end of rainspouts along the streets, symbolizing the washing away of bad fortune.

SAVANNAH GRAY BRICK

Savannah gray brick dates back to the 1800s, handmade by slaves at Hermitage Plantation, just west of the city. The gray bricks were considered less prestigious than English red brick but were always in high demand after a fire, particularly after the Civil War, when Reconstruction was an issue.

Famous Savannah homes like the Sorrel Weed House are made of Savannah gray brick, although in many cases the brick was covered over with stucco to camouflage what was considered "cheaper" building materials of the time.

The gray bricks have never been replicated today, making the remaining ones incredibly expensive. It's believed that the particular mud used to make the bricks is no longer around, and so the trademark brick style may be lost forever.

Henry Ford liked the style of the brick so well that he bought Hermitage Plantation for the sole purpose of access to the brick.

TABBY

"What's that concrete with shells in it?" The question must be asked a thousand times a day in downtown Savannah by happy visitors and locals alike. Tabby—made of equal parts lime, water sand, oyster shells and ash—is a beautiful building material dating all the way back in Savannah to the days of James Oglethorpe. He is said to have been a fan of the material, electing to use it in various structures around colonial Savannah. Tabby is usually a pale white, sometimes grayish shade of stucco-type material, with large pieces of oyster shell mixed in.

Tabby can be used in the construction of lanes and sidewalks, walls, whole buildings and, historically, fortifications. Oglethorpe became known for his tabby walls built between Georgia and the Spanish forces to the south in Florida.

Lovely colonial examples of tabby can still be found at the Wormsloe Plantation site, and even older examples are seen across the Lowcountry, especially at historic cities like Charleston and St. Augustine. Although tabby is quite lovely to look at, it hasn't been found to be the hardiest of building material. Excessive exposure to water and even vegetative overgrowth can wear away at it over time, which is why it was broadly replaced by the more modern versions of cement used today.

THE OGEECHEE CANAL SYSTEM

It's perhaps a romanticized vision of the old South—beautiful tree-draped rivers lined with moss-covered oak trees and shady pines. Ebeneezer Jenckes conceived of the idea of the canal system. In many ways, the Ogeechee Canal was a fabulous idea, one that managed to make life and the transport of goods from outlying plantations significantly easier. But it would prove to be a short-lived system.

The canal was constructed by slave laborers and more than one hundred Irish immigrants between 1826 and 1830. Completed in 1830, the working canal ran 16.5 miles, was five feet deep and forty-eight feet wide and had three wooden locks. Goods would be loaded onto small barges and then secured to mules on the edge of the water. Slaves would lead the animals up and down the canals, while the mules hauled the goods up water and into town.

The canal went bankrupt in 1836 but was bought up by investors who upgraded the old wooden locks to sturdier brick. Consequently, the canal was most prosperous between the 1840s and 1860s; the canal was used to move mostly lumber, as well as cotton, rice, Savannah gray bricks and various fruits and grains. It was a highly useful enterprise that was originally intended to connect farther up state and into Tennessee. However, the larger canal project was decommissioned due to lack of funds and topographical difficulties.

A slump in the economy during the yellow fever outbreak of 1876 took a toll on the management of the canal. Very soon after came the advancement of railroad routes to the region, and so the once acclaimed canals were almost completely out of use by the 1890s.

CATHEDRAL OF ST. JOHN THE BAPTIST

Savannah may have started as a land of opportunity for the set-upon and the minority, but it quite obviously was not a perfect system void of prejudice. Catholics were not welcome in colonial Savannah, as tensions with the Catholic Spanish raged to the south in Florida. Catholicism was declared illegal in Oglethorpe's Savannah and then barely tolerated as tension heightened toward revolution.

It was after the Siege of Savannah, when numerous Catholic French and Haitian soldiers fought and died for the people, that opposing sentiment

The Cathedral of St. John the Baptist. *Courtesy of the New York Public Library.*

started to lift. Official prejudices dissipated completely with the ratifying of the U.S. Constitution.

The congregation of St. John the Baptist met in two different smaller versions of the church over the years, beginning in 1800, up until Bishop Ignatius Persico won approval to construct a cathedral in Savannah. Construction began in November 1873 and was completed in 1876. The cathedral stood stubbornly after a fire in 1896 left it a shell of its former self and was returned to its former glory after fourteen years.

More than a century and two additional restorations later, the cathedral's two Gothic spires reach for the southern sky, beloved fixtures on the Savannah skyline. The interior is resplendent with towering stained-glass windows, intricate murals and meticulously designed Stations of the Cross. It is a shining example of Gothic architecture, the power of faith and the tenacity of the southern hearts who worship within its walls.

The Cathedral of St. John the Baptist stands as the oldest Roman Catholic Church in Georgia.

CITY MARKET

Today, visitors to Savannah's City Market will find a bustling and vibrant green lawn, bolstered on all sides by historic marketplaces, restaurants and boutiques. But not long ago, it would have been an altogether different sight.

City Market, or Ellis Square, was originally laid out in 1733, one of Oglethorpe's original four wards, then known as Decker Square for Sir Matthew Decker, one of the original Georgia Trustees. Savannah notables John and Mary Musgrove, Noble Jones and, most likely, leading physician and member of the founding Jewish community Samuel Nunes lived in the ward during Oglethorpe's time. Over the centuries, the square operated as a market area in one form or other, including a slave market from time to time. The name was changed to Ellis Square to honor Sir Henry Ellis, the second royal governor of Georgia.

Savannah's City Market in 1860. *Courtesy of the New York Public Library.*

The most interesting aspect of City Market over the years was the melting pot it proved to be within Savannah's infrastructure. Goods came into Savannah from plantations and cattle farms far and wide, attracting the full scope of the township. Members of society from all walks of life and economic backgrounds could be found there shopping and living life together.

When downtown Savannah grew quiet and neglected in the 1950s due to suburban trends, the city experimented with new ways of bringing people back into town. Unfortunately, the original City Market sat empty and was selected for demolition in favor of a parking deck. The land was reclaimed and restored to something of its original splendor in 2010.

Art and Culture

The Candler Oak

If you walk along the east end of Forsyth Park, strolling north until you come to East Gaston Street, you'll notice the live oaks, their branches sprawled up to the sky and canopied across the streets. To your right, you'll see a law school, situated within what used to be the old Candler Hospital, its proud white columns tall and freshly resplendent.

And just there, in the yard, a giant oak stands proud, its trunk thick and dark, craggly with age and centuries of bark. The Candler Oak, a Savannah treasure at the ripe age of three hundred, is one of the oldest living live oaks in Savannah. It stands at more than fifty feet tall and boasts a circumference of nearly twenty feet.

Over the years, its branches have granted shade to native Yamacraws, colonial adventurers, prisoners of war and recovering patients on strolls from the historic hospital at its back. It is now the proud logo of Savannah Law School and protected on all sides by an iron fence to ensure that it stays safe and sound.

The Candler Oak is a Georgia landmark, registered historic tree and founding project of the Savannah Tree Foundation. One would be hard-pressed to find another tree so protected or so loved by the city grown up around it.

THE SS *SAVANNAH*

The splendorous ship was built in New York, completed in 1819 and destined to operate in and out of Savannah. The SS *Savannah* was the first steamship to ever cross the Atlantic Ocean, a combination of a ship fitted with sails and side paddlewheels. Seventy-five tons of coal furnished power to the vessel, although it was intended to use the sails most of the time. The steam power was meant to be backup energy. It compares to today's hybrid cars that run on both fuel and electricity. The paddlewheels could be moved and adjusted to aid in the aerodynamics of the ship, helping to maintain or increase speed.

There were sixteen staterooms, elaborately fitted for its time, with carpet throughout the ship, curtains, bars and lounges; women's staterooms were separate and even more comfortable and luxurious. Mostly due to costs and the new technology in general, people were afraid of the project until President James Monroe sailed on the ship and enjoyed the experience.

The SS *Savannah* made its voyage across the ocean in May 1819 bound for Liverpool. It took twenty-nine days and eleven hours, relying on the steam engine for a total of eighty hours of the entire voyage.

After England, the SS *Savannah* became a worldwide wonder, visiting Sweden, Norway, Russia and Denmark before returning at last to Savannah, six months later, on November 13. It really was a masterpiece of its time.

After the fire of 1820, the owners of the ship fell on financial difficulty due to the fallout. They sold the engine of the SS *Savannah* to alleviate their debts. The *Savannah* continued on as a sailing ship until it shipwrecked off the coast of Long Island in November 1821.

FORSYTH PARK FOUNTAIN: A BEAUTIFUL CATALOGUE PIC

Perhaps one of the most iconic Savannah sights is the Forsyth Park Fountain. The stunning fountain was placed on the north end of Forsyth Park in 1858, its placement inspired by the decadent fountain centerpieces found in the parks of Paris. The citizens of Savannah had become proud of the opulence of the city's monument-adorned Bull Street. The fountain was meant to be the crown of the lane and the sparkling indicator of the newly established and evolving Forsyth Park, named for John Forsyth, Georgia's thirty-third governor.

The Forsyth Park Fountain, 1898. *Courtesy of the New York Public Library.*

The fountain arrived in its original form ordered from Janes, Beebe & Company's *Illustrated Catalogue of Ornamental Iron Work*, costing about $3,000 to install. The fountain arrived black and underwent several paint jobs and restorations over the years. It survived vandalism and extreme weather, new pump systems and pool expansions until it became the iconic sight it is today.

BROUGHTON STREET: THE ORIGINAL SHOPPING DISTRICT

Broughton Street is Georgia's first official shopping district and a constant barometer of the flow of progression and regression within Savannah's story. While today it looks like a bustling lane of commerce and fashion, over the years, it hasn't always been so.

The street was named after Governor Thomas Broughton of South Carolina in 1735 and has since proven to be one of the most consistent shopping districts in the history of the nation. George Washington visited Broughton Street on his famous trip to Savannah in 1791. The fire of 1820 left its mark, but shops were rebuilt and commerce resumed. Civil War soldiers were hospitalized there and found food and lodging during the Union occupation.

Savannah's Historic Broughton Street. *Courtesy of the New York Public Library.*

After World War II, major retailors opened branches side by side with mom and pop shops that had existed for generations. The most important thing to happen on Broughton Street was W.W. Law's peaceful protest during the civil rights movement. The protest lasted eighteen months until Savannah disbanded its segregated lunch counter policy.

As culture took a turn toward suburban life, Broughton Street quieted. Major retailers closed shops, and the historic lane fell widely into disrepair. And then, in the early 1990s, a man named Forrest sat on a bus stop bench with a box of chocolates and the world remembered downtown Savannah. And Broughton Street is once again restored, as lovely, busy and as bustling as ever.

JINGLE BELLS

There is controversy as to whether James Lord Pierpont wrote the popular Christmas tune "Jingle Bells" in Savannah or in Boston. He originally published the song as "One Horse Open Sleigh" in 1857, intending it to be a Thanksgiving song, but it was quickly adopted by the Christmas season festivities. Some say that he wrote it in Boston, based on the town's then popular sleigh races. But the copyright date of the lyrics places Pierpont in Savannah, during the time he served as music director at Savannah's Unitarian Church, now located in Savannah's Troup Square. Accordingly, Savannah lays claim to the Christmas classic.

THE SAVANNAH JAZZ SCENE

Most people associate jazz with New Orleans, but one of Savannah's most underground secrets is its jazz scene. Where Johnny Mercer brought Savannah big time swing music, Ben Tucker brought jazz.

Tucker was born in 1930 in Brentwood, Tennessee, but Savannah had his heart for forty-two years. He had a boisterous smile and a jovial laugh, and it was not uncommon to see Mr. Tucker carrying his upright bass, Bertha, his 240-year-old treasure, up Bull Street to go play the next big show. His jazz club, Hard Hearted Hanna's, is where he'd lead his jazz band six nights a week.

He performed and recorded for fifty years with artists like Benny Goodman, B.B. King, Shirley Horn and Mel Torme. He was a teacher of jazz to Savannahians through his iconic jazz radio station, WSOK, owning the number one station in Savannah for thirteen years and serving more than 400,000 listeners.

Even though he passed on after an automobile accident in 2013, his music lives on in the hearts of those who were gifted with his language of music.

THE KID BEHIND THE LEGEND: JOHNNY MERCER, SAVANNAH'S MUSIC MAN

The first family to own a car in Savannah, the owners of wealth and prestige, the Mercers are Savannah legends in their own right, but few know the story behind the Man of Moon River.

Johnny was born in 1909 to a wealthy Savannah family. His father was a lawyer who also dealt in real estate, and they lived very comfortably until 1926, when his father made a bad deal and fell under $1 million of debt. The sudden financial trouble meant that Johnny couldn't attend college, and so he ventured off to New York to try and make it as an actor.

Johnny Mercer's childhood home. *Courtesy of the Jeff Bush Photography Collection.*

He wasn't a success, but in 1933, he connected with songwriter Hoagy Carmichael. The relationship would alter his future forever. By 1933, he'd written his first hit, "Lazy Bones." Mercer moved to Hollywood, becoming a successful lyricist. He went on to found Capitol Records in 1942, eventually signing acts like Nat King Cole. He won his first of four Academy Awards in 1946. Some of his biggest songs were "Autumn Leaves," "Jeepers Creepers," "Moon River," "In the Cool Cool Cool of the Evening" and "Days of Wine and Roses."

When Johnny's father died, Johnny sold his share of Capital Records to cover the remains of his father's debts. While he never moved back to Savannah, he is interned there at Bonaventure Cemetery. A bench near his grave marker reads, "Buddy, I'm kind of a poet, and I've got a lot of things to say."

GRAYSON STADIUM

The Field of Dreams may be in Iowa, but the heart of southern baseball fans beat first in Savannah, Georgia, at Grayson Stadium. Originally named Municipal Stadium, the impressive structure was built in 1926.

Grayson Stadium has rung with the cracks of bats from Babe Ruth and Lou Gehrig. Years later, Mickey Mantle left his footprints on the field in 1957. Even Hank Aaron ran the bases within Grayson's legendary fence.

Jacki Robinson, the first black baseball player, and baseball's known villain, Ty Cobb, played at Grayson. President Roosevelt spoke at Grayson Stadium at the Georgia Bicentennial Celebration. It survived year after year of hurricanes, the strain of world wars and rising and falling economies. Today, it is home to the Savannah Bananas. Tickets sell out regularly.

THE AMERICAN GRAND PRIZE

Today, there's no international speedway to be found the likes of which are in Indianapolis or Bristol or Daytona, but on a cool November day in 1908, the first grand prix race took place in Savannah, Georgia. Back then, it was called the American Prize.

Hosted by the Savannah Automobile Club and the Automobile Club of America, the event used convict labor to build and maintain the seventeen-mile course. Extra police were called on hand to make sure convicts didn't flee, with visions of racecars screaming down the country back roads just south of the city.

Twenty cars competed, fourteen European and six American, including notable car names like Benz and Fiat and Renault. The race took place on

Thanksgiving Day, November 26, 1908. It came down to a battle among Victor Hemery, Louis Waggoner and Felice Nazzaro. Waggoner won by fifty-six seconds. The average speed was 65 miles per hour, and the fastest lap was 69.8 miles per hour. The course lasted sixteen laps, totaled 402 miles, and Louis Waggoner won in six hours, ten minutes and thirty-one seconds.

The eventual demise of the event came from public scrutiny against using convict labor to maintain the track, and accidents were common on the road during practice, resulting in one confirmed death. The final race in Savannah took place in 1911.

Once a year in November, the American Grand Prize is remembered in Savannah as racecar drivers show off their skills just across the Savannah River on Hutchison Island.

THE WAVING GIRL

Perched on the grassy edge of the Savannah River, just down the bluff from the upper Historic District stands the statue of a woman—a girl, really—her eyes trained on the water and the horizon beyond. A look of perpetual longing is on her face, and a scarf grasped in her hand waves high above her head. The Waving Girl, she's called.

Untold numbers of Savannah visitors have admired the girl over the years. But not many know the story behind the statue that greets ships day after day as they journey up the river toward port.

By the time she was nineteen, Florence Martus lived in the Elba Island Lighthouse with her brother, George. It was a taxing trip by water into town, and so short of traveling in every few weeks for supplies, Florence spent most of her time on the island. It wasn't long before she started waving at the ships—every single ship that passed by. It was a game for her, really, a way to connect with others who'd spent days separated from society by water.

Between the years of 1887 and 1931, regardless of the time of day or how hot or cold the season, Florence was there waving—for forty-four years. The sailors who frequented Savannah grew to love her, looking forward to the sight of her friendly and enthusiastic greeting. And sailors who had seen Savannah's ports had often heard of the Waving Girl and looked forward to her happy welcome as well.

Much of the mystery and lore surrounding Florence is due to the fact that she never married and seldom left the island for upward of half a century.

The Waving Girl.
*Courtesy of the Jeff
Bush Photography
Collection.*

A popular legend says she fell in love with a wayward sailor, and although he promised to return to her and marry, he never came back, leaving her heartbroken and always looking for him on each new ship that sailed by.

But Florence herself denied the truth of such legends, perhaps making her unusual and charming habit all the more mysterious. Whatever her reasoning, the famous wave became synonymous with the Hostess City and the open-heartedness that first brought Savannah to life.

Florence Martus is immortalized now, down by the water, the young woman whose heart belonged to the ocean. "Welcome," she says, "welcome to Savannah."

FLANNERY O'CONNOR

Flannery O'Connor was a literary author born in Savannah. Her birthplace sits in view of the Cathedral of St. John the Baptist, its two large spires reaching for the sky. Her stories abound with religious undertones and symbolic commentary on the oddities and contrasts of life and the sinful underbelly of human nature. The house is a narrow townhome, where she lived with her parents until the age of thirteen, when her family moved to Milledgeville. Many believe it was her childhood years in the colorful city that inspired much of her work. Today, fans of her work can tour her childhood home, now a museum.

Literary author Flannery O'Connor's childhood home. *Courtesy of the Jeff Bush Photography Collection.*

SAVANNAH'S DARK SIDE

THE CITY BUILT ON ITS DEAD

There are many hidden cemeteries of Savannah. Savannah started out small, and as it grew, more than a few cemeteries became the foundation to some of the city's most frequented locals, not to mention squares and homes. Charleston is called the Holy City because of its churches. Williamsburg, Virginia, is said to be haunted. Savannah is known as the City Built on Its Dead.

As a meticulously planned city, there wasn't much thought put into burying the dead far beyond the constraints of town, so as Savannah grew, the dead weren't moved—they were just built on top of. Savannah's very first cemetery was established in 1733 and was used until 1750, situated at the intersections of Whitaker and Bull and West York Street and Oglethorpe Avenue. It's a hub of activity there today, adjacent to one of the historic district's most popular squares, and on the land sits historic apartment buildings, shopping boutiques and restaurants. The dead are there, lying below the hum of life above. And so the story goes, on and on within the historic district and its many hidden cemeteries. It's this distinction that many believe led to Savannah earning the title of the nation's most haunted city.

Time and again, home renovators and gardeners have come across human bones while digging not so far from the surface. Not to speak of larger construction projects that have encountered strange delays to allow archaeologists to come exhume and document the latest discovery of historic remains.

SAVANNAH'S FIRST MURDER

What do you get when an indentured servant is driven to the edge by her master? Savannah's first murder. It was the beginning of a colony, the first breath of Oglethorpe's long-awaited new life across the ocean. The men and women who'd accompanied him on the ship *Anne* and braved two months of harrowing travel had finally settled into what resembled a routine. Individuals had been granted plots of land, responsibilities had been doled out and indentured servants had been assigned their masters. It was a time of adjustment in the most uncomfortable sense of the word.

The humid, cold winter, wildlife and marshy, wild terrain were the order of the day. The work was physical and draining, cutting trees and clearing land for their settlement. Lumber was moved and stacked by hand, and small, rustic cabins were assembled in group efforts, racing against the cold to secure warm, reasonably safe shelter.

Among the settlers was a man named William Wise. He was a known scoundrel, having been caught trying to sneak a prostitute aboard the ship to accompany him to the New World. Gruff and generally avoided, he was granted the land a stone's throw across the Savannah River, on what now is known as Hutchison Island. And two indentured servants were granted him to help with the establishment of his plot, Alice Riley and Richard White.

There has been conjecture that Alice and Richard were romantically involved. Both of them were young and vibrant, Alice with long dark hair and apparent bravado given her current circumstances. Not much is known about Richard, save for his assumed feelings toward Alice.

The story goes that William Wise requested nightly sponge baths from Alice, culminating in her washing his hair in a basin as he reclined on the bed. Night after night, she was compelled to the less-than-desirable work, and many believe that William was taking unwanted physical liberties with Alice.

It wasn't long before a plan was in place. The night of his murder, William reclined on the bed as Alice washed his hair. Only this time, Richard was waiting in the wings. He and Alice overtook William, submerging his head and drowning him in his own wash basin.

Perhaps it was a premeditated plan to escape the settlement and make a run for Charleston. Perhaps it was a crime of passion or self-defense. Whatever the situation, Alice and Richard knew what they had done. They ran, stealing away in the night in an attempt to disappear in the marshland. The two were tracked down, though, and brought before the leaders of Savannah.

Richard was found guilty of murder and hanged the same day in Wright Square—the "Justice Square," as it came to be known. Alice was found guilty as well. But she had a secret. When she announced her pregnancy, there was question as to which of the men was the baby's father. What wasn't up for debate was that they couldn't hang a pregnant woman.

Nine months they waited. When the child was born, it was whisked away from its mother, and Alice was marched to the gallows. The crime and punishment was a premonition of the dramatic future that lay ahead for Savannah. Nothing would ever appear straightforward, it seemed. Drama waited for the small settlement at every turn.

They Hoodoo Voodoo

Chances are when most people think of voodoo, they think of New Orleans. But when they think of hoodoo, they should think of Savannah, Georgia.

What's the difference? Voodoo is technically an official religion that calls on the power of African gods. Hoodoo, on the other hand, is a practice based in folklore that mixes in many ways with both Catholic traditions and voodoo principles. An amalgamation of religion and culture that grew out of the influence of African slaves who ultimately settled primarily just off of coastal Georgia, hoodoo is still alive and well in Savannah and the surrounding region, although most locals go about their lives completely unaware of it.

They're called hoodoo root doctors or root workers. They conjure the spirits of the dead to rise up to do either good or evil. If someone in your family wants to fall in love, you would hire a hoodoo root doctor to help. The doctor would go to the cemetery, locate someone who enjoyed a long and happy marriage in life and purchase a bit of the grave site dirt of the person. It's called "buying graveyard dirt." They purchase the dirt with a bit of silver or whiskey that they leave there at the grave and then take the dirt they need. They would then use that dirt to cast a spell and usher in loving energy and attraction to their paying client. The same such spells could be used for curses as well.

If someone in your family starts suffering from bad luck, one of the first things they would have done would be to go and look in their yard for any sign of something having been buried, as hoodoo curses were often given as dark and sometimes poisonous packages buried in the victim's yard.

YELLOW FEVER

Savannah was host to all sorts of visitors over the years. People from far and wide frequented its shores, a thriving port. But the city's coastal positioning was also one of its most unexpected and unfortunate challenges. The marshy, humid surroundings proved to be the perfect atmosphere for mosquitos. Little was understood about many diseases at the time, particularly how diseases traveled and were communicated. Mosquitoes and gnats and marsh pests were nothing new. Residents generally accepted them as a fact of life and paid them little heed.

It was 1820 when yellow fever first reared its ugly head in Savannah. It spread like wildfire, and no one knew exactly how or why. It was assumed at first that the disease was spread from person to person, and so once a family member came down with symptoms, they were immediately quarantined inside the house.

Yellow fever was a terrible ailment. They called it the "Stranger's Disease" because seemingly the originators came from the general direction of the port. Once infected, victims came down with muscle aches, headaches, stomach troubles and jaundice. For a few, that was as bad as it got. But unfortunately for most, the disease worsened, bringing on insatiable thirst, fever, furry tongue, swollen lips, delirious episodes and vomiting bile. It was this last bit that harkened internal bleeding and impending death. By the time the disease abated, one-tenth of Savannah's population had fallen victim. Two more epidemics followed, one in 1854 and the worst of them all in 1876 after a torrentially wet spring season.

Treatment was primarily experimental. They tried bleeding patients by issuing a series of small cuts on the arm and squeezing what they believed to be infected blood into bowls. This unfortunate practice only served to weaken their patients further. A multitude of other treatments, including doses of sulfur and arsenic, were administered as doctors worked exhaustively to try and turn the tide. Doctors came from far and wide to lend their services as the epidemic had garnered national attention.

As found in James R. Gruenberg's "The Yellow Fever Epidemic in Savannah, Georgia, of 1876," volunteer Dr. Falligent famously said in 1876, "By the first week in September the cloud of suffering hung like a pall over every district, and misery and woe found echo only in the wail of the mourner and the thud of the coffin." As it had in the past, the fever mysteriously abated with the coming of the winter months. It wasn't until the early twentieth century that mosquitos were discovered to be the source of yellow fever.

DEAD RINGERS

They say one of the most visceral phobias a person can have is being buried alive—to wake in the dark of the pitch black, reach out your hand and find yourself contained in a box. To smell the earth and musty dirt, trapped with no hope of escape.

It's a terrifying scenario and, unfortunately, one that used to play out all too often. Medical knowledge was severely limited when it came to sicknesses and fevers that left sufferers in comas. People were buried by accident all the time. The practice of holding wakes became popular. A deceased family member would be laid in state in the front parlor, for several days in most cases, just to be absolutely certain that death had taken them.

But even these measures weren't perfect, especially in the case of what they believed at the time to be catching illnesses, like yellow fever. Deceased loved ones would be removed from the house much sooner, sometimes taken to mass graves or family crypts with hardly any waiting at all.

The unfortunate victims would be interred. But then another family member would catch the fever and pass away as quickly as the first. When that victim was taken to the same crypt, lo and behold, the family member before them would be found not lying in state on the shelf where they'd been placed but sprawled out on the ground, dead from starvation and exposure and fear.

It became something of a trend. Families and individuals became paranoid and worried that they themselves or a loved one might come to suffer such a fate. It was such a legitimate fear that George Washington himself was watched closely for two days after his death, and extra breathing tubes were run from above ground and into his coffin just in case.

And things started to get interesting. You'll hear various popular phrases associated with graveyard history: "dead ringer," "graveyard shift" and "saved by the bell." However, none of those phrases actually came from graveyards. "Dead ringer" was a nineteenth-century phrase used by bookies before horse races, describing how they'd showcase an identical horse before the race to confuse betters. The look-alike horses were called dead ringers. The phrase "graveyard shift" simply sprang from the description of late-night working, usually between 11:00 p.m. and 10:00 a.m. Simple as that. "Saved by the bell" is boxing slang, originating in 1893.

This brings us back to the graveyards. A bell would be hung outside the coffin or tomb, attached to a rope; the rope would then wind into the coffin and wrap around the wrist of the corpse. The night watchman's job was to

Colonial Park Cemetery, Savannah, Georgia. *Courtesy of the New York Public Library.*

keep an ear out for the bell, run like mad to locate its origin and dig up the terrified person.

One unique patent was by Franz Vester in 1868 New Jersey. Franz patented the glass screen to a coffin. If the person was initially laid to rest in the church, the night watchman could either hear the bell or look down and see the condensation of breath on the glass or see if a corpse had moved or shifted in their coffin.

Today at Savannah's Bonaventure Cemetery, the grave of Charles F. Mills still boasts a bell sticking up from the ground.

THE BURNING OF SAVANNAH

It was November 26, 1796, and Savannah had finally recovered from the carnage of the Revolution. There was renewed energy and hope alive in the city. At that time, Savannah wasn't yet much bigger than Oglethorpe's original layout, with six city squares making up the bulk of the township. It had been a particularly dry summer, and most of the buildings were still constructed of wood. A bakery fire began in the early morning hours, and by lunchtime, it had nearly leveled the city, leaving four hundred families homeless in its wake. The fire served as a leveling of culture as well, with rich and poor suddenly back on common ground. Rebuilding efforts saw the city once again on its feet by 1798.

Fire struck Savannah again on January 11, 1820. This time, it was suspected arson at Boone's Livery Stable. The building caught fire, and the flames spread rapidly to City Market, where kegs of gunpowder were being illegally stored. The ensuing explosion destroyed 463 buildings. The fire raged for twelve hours, through the night until midday the next day.

Finally, in 1825, Savannah's first organized fire department was established, composed of twenty employees made up of both enslaved and freed African Americans. By 1826, firemen were paid $1.21 per hour once arriving to the scene of the fire. The first slave to arrive on the scene received an extra dollar's pay.

There was a fire that struck Savannah on January 27, 1865, during Sherman's occupation of the city, destroying one hundred buildings in the district. Union soldiers were suspected to be the cause. The fire was extinguished following the explosion of an ammunitions facility. The fire wasn't ordered to be set by Sherman or any of the other generals.

In 1870, advanced firefighting systems were put into use, including nineteen telegraph boxes installed throughout the city meant for residents to report fires.

The burning of Savannah, 1820. *Courtesy of the New York Public Library.*

MARSHALL HOUSE HOTEL: A CIVIL WAR HOSPITAL

The Marshall House was built in 1851 by Mary Marshall after being left the Broughton Street land by her father. Her dream had always been to own a hotel. Over the years, the hotel saw many changes and went through many owners. In 1940, it became the Gilbert House, and balconies were added to the front of the building. It fell into disrepair in the late 1950s and became nearly unrecognizable, remaining that way until the 1990s, when it was bought in 1998 by a group of investors and renovated to its original splendor, balconies included.

The building has since won numerous historical awards for the renovation and attention to detail. But as far as history, the Marshall House is one of the most significant historic markers in Savannah history, particularly during the Civil War. When Sherman took the city of Savannah after burning Atlanta to the ground, he spared the city in favor of rest and recovery for him and his men. The Marshall House was used as his Union hospital. Mr. Herbert Gilbert was the owner at the time.

Sixty-five thousand troops were in Savannah during its occupation, and the Marshall House paid host to many of them while they were here. The house was primarily used for surgeries and amputations. A male nurse would enter

The Marshall House Hotel, 1865. *Courtesy of the New York Public Library.*

the room of a new patient, hand them a bottle of liquor and say, "Drink it up." Once the young man was thoroughly drunk, he'd be escorted downstairs, where he'd be met with the sound of screams and moaning. The air would smell like blood and decay. None of the original splendor of the Marshall House remained. The soldier would be laid on the unclean table. The doctor would take out his leather tourniquets, a bullet for the soldier to bite on and his bone saw. And from there, the surgery began.

This was wartime, so laudanum was in short supply. If the soldier could make it through the amputation, that was half the battle. Once the limb was removed several minutes later, the doctor would stuff what was left of the appendage with sawdust and lint, cauterize and bind up the wound and call for the next patient. Miraculously, many of the soldiers managed to survive recovery.

The Marshall House recovered, of course, as did the rest of the city. But Savannah was struck with outbreaks of yellow fever in 1854 and 1876, and the Marshall House was called on again as a hospital for the sick and dying.

The number of people who've actually died in the hotel is not clear. Years later, bones were discovered under the floors during the 1990s renovation. The hotel is now a luxury haven for visitors to Savannah and also enjoys the title of one of the most haunted hotels in the country.

CORRINE ELLIOT LAWTON

One of Savannah's most popular star-crossed legends claims that Corrine Elliot Lawton, the daughter of a Civil War brigadier general, threw herself into the Savannah River and drowned rather than marry the man chosen for her by her parents.

The young woman's haunting memorial statue is said to be a remarkable likeness of the thirty-one-year-old, who died on the eve of her wedding. The sculpture's eyes are vacant and sad. Her gravestone reads, "Allured to brighter worlds, and led the way." The legend claims that her family never forgave her for the suicide, burying her with her sculpture's back facing the family plot.

However, historical records, including Lawton's official obituary, contradict the legend. There's no mention of a suicide or even a suicide attempt. Her mother's diary records Corrine's death as the result of a sudden weeklong illness, noting that she passed away in her home, surrounded by loving family.

As for the positioning of her memorial, with her sculpture's back facing away from her family's plot, Corrine was originally buried at Savannah's Laurel Grove Cemetery, and then her remains were moved to Bonaventure with the rest of her family years later. There is no confirmed significance behind her memorial's positioning.

THE GRIBBLE HOUSE

The Gribble House, which used to sit at 401 West Perry Street, was the scene of one of Savannah's most horrific crimes. On December 10, 1909, Eliza Gribble and her daughter, Carrie, were discovered dead in the house, along with Maggie Hunter, who was found terribly beaten and died later.

Maggie had just moved into the house the day before, renting a room from Mrs. Gribble. Maggie was found at the front door, her throat slit and her head beaten in. The crime was reported that same day, making national news almost right away and resulting in mobs and rioting as the men of Savannah rounded up suspects.

That night in the hospital before Maggie died, she confided to a priest that her husband, J.C. Hunter, was the attacker. He was immediately arrested, along with a man named Willie Wallace and John Coker. The men pleaded not guilty, but J.C. Hunter was found guilty and sentenced to death by hanging. All the way up until his execution date on December 22, 1911, he insisted that he was innocent of the crime. The day before his execution, the judge had a change of heart and sentenced Hunter instead to life in prison. However, on October 27, 1923, he was pardoned and set free.

The Gribble House was torn down in 1944.

CONRAD AIKEN

Literary giant Conrad Aiken hailed from Savannah, but very few know the dark and tragic history of his childhood that inspired his famous work.

It was a night much like any other in Savannah. Conrad was the oldest of four children, asleep in his bed on the early morning of February 27, 1901. He was woken up before the sun rose by his father, William, who was down the hallway having a heated discussion with Conrad's mother, Anna. While he listened, Conrad heard his father say, "One, two, three." *Pow. Pow.* Two gunshots.

Conrad climbed out of bed to go see what had happened. As he opened the door, he found his father and mother on the floor, shot dead. Conrad immediately ran out of the house and straight for the police station, adjacent to Colonial Park Cemetery.

The police ran back to the house with Conrad and, following an investigation, determined it was a murder-suicide. After their parents' deaths, Conrad and his siblings were adopted by distant relatives in New England. Throughout the years, people hoped that he would turn out okay. He was a smart young man, doing well in school and going on to attend Harvard, where he met his close friend and fellow writer T.S. Elliot.

Conrad became a writer known for his dark poetry, going on to win a Pulitzer in 1930. He wrote of himself in *Ushant*, "After the desultory early-morning quarrel, came the half-stifled scream, the sound of his father's voice counting three, and the two loud pistol shots and he tiptoed into the dark room, where the two bodies lay motionless, and apart, and finding them dead, found himself possessed of them forever."

He went on to live a tumultuous life, married three times and battled affairs, anxiety and suicide attempts. He found himself in 1962 back in Savannah, where he lived out the final eleven years of his life in the house next door to where his parents died. He was at Bonaventure Cemetery one day, visiting the graves of his parents. He saw a ship on the river in the distance and read the name to be the *Cosmos Mariner*. He was intrigued with the name and spent some days trying to determine where the ship had come from and where it was going. He was never able to find any details other than its name, destination unknown.

The poetry was not lost on him. He's buried now at Bonaventure, his grave marked with the words, "Cosmos Mariner, destination unknown."

BONAVENTURE CEMETERY: THE STORY BENEATH THE GRAVEYARD

Sitting just a stone's throw outside of Savannah's Historic District lies a location slightly less visited, but the history here is as dramatic and interesting as the heart of Savannah itself.

Bonaventure Cemetery, Savannah, Georgia, 1898. *Courtesy of the New York Public Library.*

The cemetery has its roots as Bonaventure Plantation, established during the trustee age of Savannah, when John Mullryne claimed the area for himself and his family in 1764. He put the land in his wife's name. By the time he finished buying up land in adjoining areas, he had expanded Bonaventure Plantation to more than six hundred acres. Mullryne went on to be highly active in Georgia politics, up until the time of the Revolution. A British Loyalist, John Mullryne aided fellow Loyalist Governor Wright in his escape out of Savannah at the height of Revolutionary tension, smuggling him across Bonaventure Plantation to waiting British forces at sea.

The plantation was used for treating the wounded after the Siege of Savannah, and after the Revolution, the Mullrynes were driven out of the city for their British sympathies. The plantation eventually came up for auction and was purchased by John Habersham, the Revolutionary son of James Habersham, as a means to extend his holdings in Savannah. It was eventually bought back by decedents of the original owners and stayed in the family until it became too much to manage following a plantation house fire.

In June 1868, the plantation was purchased by Savannah businessman Peter Wiltberger, whose family parceled the land into Evergreen Cemetery. Savannah residents were able to bury their loved ones there but also used the picturesque place to enjoy picnics, morning promenades and even weddings.

The cemetery was bought by the City of Savannah and renamed Bonaventure Cemetery in July 1907. Over the years, Bonaventure has been a source of fascination and wonder to both Savannah natives and travelers alike. It's a place of death and sadness, remembrance and reverence, draped on all sides by sleepy, moss-covered oak trees, azalea bushes and shady grass. The meandering Wilmington River kisses the cemetery's edge, the soft hush of flowing water a quiet reminder of the passing of time—of the world moving on beyond Bonaventure's gates.

Today, visitors can pay respects to the graves of notable cemetery residents such as Johnny Mercer, Conrad Aiken, Noble Jones and many more.

BIBLIOGRAPHY

Aiken, Conrad. *Ushant.* New York: Oxford University Press, 1971.

Appleton, D. "Wilson, James Grant; Fiske, John, eds. (1900), McIntosh, Lachlan." *Appleton's Encyclopedia of American Biography.* New York, n.d.

Babb, Tara. "'Without a Few Negroes': George Whitefield, James Habersham, and Bethesda Orphan House in the Story of Legalizing Slavery in Colonial Georgia." Thesis, University of South Carolina, 2009.

Bell, Karen. "Atlantic Slave Trade to Savannah." *New Georgia Encyclopedia,* August 5, 2015.

Belzer, Mark Arnold, and B.H. Levy. "Virtual Jewish World: Savannah, Georgia." Jewish Virtual Library. www.jewishvirtuallibrary.org.

Berry, Daina, and Lisa M. Harris. *Slavery and Freedom in Savannah.* Athens: University of Georgia Press, 2014.

Berry, Daina, Leslie Harris and Joan Neuberger. "Urban Slavery in the Antebellum United States." *15 Minute History, Not Even Past* (podcast), episode no. 54, September 17, 2014.

Braddock, J.G., Sr. "The Man Who Invented Georgia." Wooden Ships, Iron Men, 2012. http://woodenshipsironmen.com.

Brooks, Lacey Elizabeth. "Municipal Slavery: The City of Savannah's Ownership of Enslaved People." April 2014. savannahga.gov.

Brown, Brian. "Savannah—Ogeechee Canal, 1830." *Vanishing Coastal Georgia,* February 4, 2018.

Burke, Maureen, and Connie Capozzola Pinkerton. *The Savannah College of Art and Design: Restoration of an Architectural Heritage.* Charleston, SC: Arcadia Publishing, 2004.

Cashin, Edward J. "Royal Georgia, 1752–1776." *New Georgia Encyclopedia*, June 8, 2017.

———. "Trustee Georgia, 1732–1752." *New Georgia Encyclopedia*, September 2, 2015.

Cleveland, Henry. *Alexander H. Stephens, in Public and Private: With Letters and Speeches, Before, During, and Since the War*. Philadelphia, PA, 1886.

Colquitt, Adrian. "Forsyth Park, Savannah's Lovely Centerpiece Filled with Interest." *Savannah Morning News*, 1928.

Congressional record, vol. 135 (2009). *111th Congress Public Law* 94. Joint Resolution.

Coulter, E. Merton. *Wormsloe: Two Centuries of a Georgia Family*. Athens: University of Georgia Press, 1955.

Cox, Dale. "The Battle of Gully Hole Creek–St. Simons Island, Georgia." Explore Southern History, 2011. exploresouthernhistory.com.

———. "Fort Darien Historical Marker—Darien, Georgia: Fort of the Highland Scots." Explore Southern History, January 2014. exploresouthernhistory.com.

Deaton, Stan. "James Wright (1716–1785)." *New Georgia Encyclopedia*, February 21, 2018.

Dembling, Sophia. "Saving Savannah: The Preservation Legacy of Anna Colquitt Hunter." National Trust for Historic Preservation, 2015. savingplaces.org.

DeScanctis, Francesca. "Pin Point Community." Georgia Historical Society, 2014.

Douglass, Frederick. *The Narrative of the Life of Frederick Douglass an American Slave*. Boston: published at the Anti-Slavery Office, 1849.

Elmore, Charles J. "W.W. Law (1923–2002)." *New Georgia Encyclopedia*, February 12, 2016.

Erazo, Laura. "Savannah's First Newspaper." Georgia Historical Society, The Hidden History Project, 2016.

Ewing, Joseph H. "The New Sherman Letters." *American Heritage* 38, no. 5 (July–August 1987).

Flanagan, Kelly. Georgia Historical Society, 2014. georgiahistoricalsociety. com.

Frank, Andrew K. "Mary Musgrove (ca. 1700–ca. 1763)." *New Georgia Encyclopedia*, February 21, 2018.

Frasier, Walter J. *Savannah in the Old South*. Athens: University of Georgia Press, 2003.

Georgia Historical Society. "Chatham Artilleries Washington Guns." N.d.

———. "Mother Mathilda Beasley." georgiahistory.com.

Goellnitz, Jenny. "Civil War Battlefield Surgery." https://ehistory.osu.edu/exhibitions/cwsurgeon/cwsurgeon/amputations.

Gordon, Sarah. "Flannery O'Connor (1925–1964)." *New Georgia Encyclopedia*, July 26, 2017.

Green, Michael D. "Mary Musgrove Creating a New World." In *Sifters: Native American Women's Lives*. Edited by Theda Perdue. New York: Oxford University Press, 2001.

Gruenberg, James R. "The Yellow Fever Epidemic in Savannah, Georgia, of 1876: A Case for Applied Historical Analysis." Thesis, Wright State University, 2012.

Habersham, Josephine Clay. *Habersham Diary*, #1264-z. Southern Historical Collection, The Wilson Library, University of North Carolina–Chapel Hill.

Hancock, Daniel. "Bonaventure: From Plantation to Monument." Bonaventure Historical Society. YouTube, January 18, 2017.

Hatfield, Edward A. "First African Baptist Church." *New Georgia Encyclopedia*, June 6, 2017.

Jackson, Edwin L. "James Oglethorpe (1696–1785)." *New Georgia Encyclopedia*, February 21, 2018.

Jones, Charles Colcock. *The History of Georgia: Aboriginal and Colonial Epochs*. Boston: Houghton, Mifflin and Company, 1883.

"Jruffinsr." "Preview History of First African Baptist Church Savannah GA." YouTube, January 22, 2008.

Keber, Martha, and Charles Elmore. "World War II and Savannah Shipyards." CSPAN, video, June 7, 2011.

Lane, Mills, ed. "In Their Own Words, February 10, 1733—Oglethorpe Letter to Trustees." *General Oglethorpe's Georgia: Colonial Letters, 1733–1743*. Savannah, GA: Beehive Press, 1990.

Lang, Leona. "African History Spotlight: A History Lesson on the Great Community of Frogtown." *Savannah Herald*, 2015. savannahherald.net.

Lechner, Alison. "The Waving Girl." Georgia Historical Society. georgiahistory.com.

Lynch, Wayne. "Button Gwinnett and Lachlan McIntosh Duel." *Journal of the American Revolution* (September 24, 2014).

Manning, Jack. "Pulaski Is Born." *American Patriotic Chronicle*, March 6, 2017.

Miller, Steven F. "Newspaper Account of a Meeting between Black Religious Leaders and Union Military Authorities." Freedmen & Southern Society Project, December 10, 2017.

Mills, Lane, ed. *General Oglethorpe's Georgia: Colonial Letters, 1733–1743.* Vol. 1. Savannah, GA: Beehive Press, 1990.

Mufwene, Salikoko Sangol. "Gullah." *Encyclopedia Britannica,* July 25, 2016.

Myers, Barton. "Sherman's Field Order No. 15." *New Georgia Encyclopedia,* June 8, 2017.

Nate D. Sanders Auctions. "Button Gwinnett's Signature." Los Angeles, 2017.

The National Archives. "From George Washington to Savannah Officials." May 13–14, 1791. founders.archives.gov.

Online Georgia Almanac. "The Georgia Hussars." Georgia Historic Marker.

———. "John Reynolds." University of Georgia Library. https://www.libs.uga.edu.

PBS. "The Weeping Time: Africans in America." *Judgement Day,* Part 4. www.pbs.org.

Polascak, Marissa. "History of the Gullah Culture." Pawleys Island, South Carolina, July 6, 2015. pawleysisland.com.

Runyon, Shane A. "Malcontents." *New Georgia Encyclopedia,* September 2, 2015.

Russel, Preston, and Barbara Hines. "Savannah: A History of Her People Since 1733." N.p.: Frederic C. Beil, publisher, 1992.

Sweet, Julie A. "Tomochichi (ca. 1644–1739)." *New Georgia Encyclopedia,* February 21, 2018.

Twohig, Dorothy, Mark A. Mastromarino and Jack D. Warren, eds. *The Papers of George Washington.* Presidential Series. Vol. 5, January 16, 1790–June 30, 1790. Charlottesville: University Press of Virginia, 1996.

Underwood, John Levi. *The Women of the Confederacy: In Which Is Presented the Heroism of the Women of the Confederacy with Accounts of Their Trials During the War and the Period of the Reconstruction, with Their Ultimate Triumph Over Adversity, Their Motives and Achievements as Told by Writers and Orators Now Preserved in Permanent Form.* N.p.: Neale Publishing Company, 1906.

U.S. War Department. *The War of the Rebellion: A Compilation of the Official Records of the Union and Confederate Armies.* Series I, vol. 44. Washington, D.C.: U.S. Government Printing Office, 1893. Reprinted by the National Historical Society, 1971.

Ware, Gabrielle. "Savannah Residents Remember Frogtown and Old West Broad Street." GPB Media, October 13, 2015. www.gpb.org/news/2015/10/13/savannah-residents-remember-frogtown-and-old-west-broad-street.

White, Meghan. "This Bar's Unusual Architecture Preserves Part of Georgia's History." Saving Places, 2017. savingplaces.org.

Williams, Arden. "Catharine Greene (1755–1814)." *New Georgia Encyclopedia*, November 12, 2013.

Withun, David. "Beasley, Mother Mathilda (1832–1903)." Black Past, n.d. blackpast.org.

Worthha, Karen. "Underground Railroad History Fills the Pews." *Savannah Now*, 2007. savannahnow.com.

Zainaldin, Jamil S. "Great Depression." *New Georgia Encyclopedia*, April 17, 2018.

About the Authors

BRENNA MICHAELS holds an MFA in writing popular fiction from Seton Hill University. In addition to her work as a southern fiction novelist, she is senior editor of the *Genteel & Bard Journal*.

TIMOTHY MICHAELS is a retired actor and radio host whose career took him from Los Angeles to Nashville's Grand Ole Opry, Atlanta and, finally, the Emerald Coast of Savannah. Timothy holds a BFA in acting from the North Carolina School of the Arts.

Brenna and T.C. Michaels are professional storytellers, public historians and owners of Genteel & Bard, a Luxury Southern Lifestyle and Touring Company—curating bespoke and luxury multimedia experiences. They live in Savannah's historic district. Mint juleps have been known to happen.

Visit us at
www.historypress.com